Lauren McWade

INTERMEDIATE 1
English

Jane Cooper and **Annie Rayner**

Close Reading Consultant: **Ann Bridges**

Hodder Gibson

A MEMBER OF THE HODDER HEADLINE GROUP

The Publishers would like to thank the following for permission to reproduce copyright material:

Photo credits   Page 12 © Imperial War Museum/Q11596; page 34 © David Moir/The Scotsman; page 37 © David Kilpatrick/Alamy; page 53 © Tim de Waele/Corbis; page 94 © Ronald Grant Archive; page 155 © Michael Boyd/PA/EMPICS; page 229 © Keith M Law/Alamy

Acknowledgements   Artworks by Emma Golley/IFA Design Ltd.

Extracts from 'The Jaguar' by Ted Hughes reprinted by permission of Faber and Faber; *Stone Cold* reproduced by permission of the Penguin Group. Copyright © Robert Swindells, 1993; from *Private Peaceful* reprinted by permission of HarperCollins Publishers Ltd. © Michael Morpurgo 2003; article by Edward Black reprinted by permission of The Scotsman; Chattering Classes article reproduced by permission of the Times Educational Supplement; article by Rosie Brown reprinted by permission of Sunday Herald, Fresh Magazine; *Radio Times* article reprinted by permission of Sharon Maxwell Magnus; from *Neither Here Nor There* © Bill Bryson. Extracted from NEITHER HERE NOR THERE by Bill Bryson, published by Black Swan, a division of Transworld Publishers. All rights reserved; from *It's Not About the Bike: My Journey Back to Life* by Lance Armstrong, published by Yellow Jersey Press. Reprinted by permission of The Random House Group Ltd; from *Toast* reprinted by permission of HarperCollins Publishers Ltd. © Nigel Slater 2003; from *Lamb to the Slaughter* © Roald Dahl reproduced by permission of David Higham Associates Limited; from 'Child on Top of a Greenhouse' and 'My Papa's Waltz' by Theodore Roethke reprinted by permission of Faber and Faber; 'The Identification' by Roger McGough from Gig (Copyright © Roger McGough 1973) is reproduced by permission of PFD (www.pfd.co.uk) on behalf of Roger McGough; from Hideous Kinky by permission of Penguin Books Ltd, © Esther Freud, 1992; from exam papers and SQA letters reprinted by permission of the Scottish Qualifications Authority.

Every effort has been made to trace all copyright holders, but if any have been inadvertently overlooked the Publishers will be pleased to make the necessary arrangements at the first opportunity.

Although every effort has been made to ensure that website addresses are correct at time of going to press, Hodder Gibson cannot be held responsible for the content of any website mentioned in this book. It is sometimes possible to find a relocated web page by typing in the address of the home page for a website in the URL window of your browser.

Orders: please contact Bookpoint Ltd, 130 Milton Park, Abingdon, Oxon OX14 4SB. Telephone: (44) 01235 827720. Fax: (44) 01235 400454. Lines are open from 9.00 – 6.00, Monday to Saturday, with a 24-hour message answering service. Visit our website at www.hoddereducation.co.uk. Hodder Gibson can be contacted direct on: Tel: 0141 848 1609; Fax: 0141 889 6315; email: hoddergibson@hodder.co.uk

© Jane Cooper and Annie Rayner 2006
First published in 2006 by
Hodder Gibson, a member of the Hodder Headline Group
2a Christie Street
Paisley PA1 1NB

ISBN-10: 0 340-91473-4
ISBN-13: 978-0-340-91473-1

Impression number   10 9 8 7 6 5 4 3 2 1
Year   2010   2009   2008   2007   2006

With Answers version
ISBN-10: 0 340-92645-7
ISBN-13: 978-0-340-92645-1

Impression number   10 9 8 7 6 5 4 3 2 1
Year   2010   2009   2008   2007   2006

Cover photo by Isaac Newman/Alamy
Typeset in 12 on 14pt Bembo by Phoenix Photosetting, Lordswood, Chatham, Kent
Printed and bound in Italy

A catalogue record for this title is available from the British Library

Introduction

The Intermediate 1 course gives you many opportunities to display your English skills. You will be assessed in class and also by an exam at the end of the course.

The assessments you tackle in class are usually called **NABs** (National Assessment Banks). There are four of these. You can do these NABs in any order, and your teacher will decide when you are ready to try each one. They are:

- **Textual Analysis**, in which you are given a short piece of literature text you have never seen before and have to analyse the writer's skills and techniques

- **Close Reading**, in which you read a short passage of non-fiction and answer questions on it

- the **Personal Study**, in which you choose a book to study, and then plan and write an essay about it

- **Writing**, in which you plan and produce a story, a piece of personal writing, a discursive piece or some other piece of writing.

Once you have passed all the NABs you'll be ready for the exam, which will be in mid-May. There are two short exam papers:

- **Close Reading**, in which, as with the NAB, you'll read a short non-fiction passage and answer questions on it

- the **Critical Essay**, in which you write an essay about a literature text you have studied in class.

This book contains everything you need for a complete Intermediate 1 English course. It even includes three poems and three short stories you can study to prepare for the critical essay in the exam. (Your teacher may also use other literature texts, perhaps a play or a novel.) The Close Reading and Textual Analysis passages used in this book have been shortened here. You might like to read them in full by finding the books that the extracts come from in your library.

Once you've finished this course you may want to go on to Intermediate 2 or Higher. These courses are harder, but they do follow the same structure as Intermediate 1 and assess the same skills, so what you're about to do now will be a good preparation for the future too.

1 Textual Analysis

During class time, you will have to pass a NAB called **Textual Analysis**. This will be based on an extract from a short story, novel or play, or perhaps on a whole short poem. You will have to read the text carefully, and then answer questions on **how** it is written – the skill of the writer in choosing the words to use, and the best way to put them together. You will be doing **analysis** of a **text** – **Textual Analysis**. You must pass this NAB in order to pass the course.

The skills you learn will also be useful in the Close Reading NAB which you also have to pass, and in the final Close Reading exam, where some questions will be marked with an **A** to show they are testing your analysis skills. About half the marks in the Close Reading part of the final exam will be for analysis questions.

Sometimes in Intermediate 1, you will get marks for a very basic answer – but you are going to learn to give good, full answers here because you will want to gain the maximum number of marks. It is also likely you will want to go on to do Intermediate 2 or Higher in the future, and in these you *must* give full answers. You might as well learn to do this from the start.

First, a bit of reassurance, and a bit of revision. You've actually done quite a lot of Textual Analysis in the past, although it may not have been called that.

Textual Analysis just means **analysing** or looking closely at a text to see how the writer conveys or gets across a message to you, the reader. Writers choose every single word very carefully. They use a number of **language techniques**, which are the tricks or skills of the writer's trade. These techniques are also sometimes called the **features** or **aspects** of the text, or they may just be things in the text that you are asked about.

In this chapter you will learn to look carefully at the writer's:

- **word choice**: the words the writer chooses to use
- **structure**: the way the writer **constructs** or builds up his sentences, or paragraphs, or the whole poem or story.

There are some other **language techniques** writers use when they want to describe things vividly:

- **imagery**: for example **simile, metaphor** and **personification**, in which the writer describes something by **comparing** it to something else, giving you a vivid **image** or picture in your mind
- **alliteration** and **onomatopoeia** and some other techniques in which the **sound** of the words chosen is important.

Just to remind you what these mean, we'll revise them using examples from the poem *The Jaguar* by Ted Hughes. In this poem Hughes writes about a scene at a zoo where all the animals are sleeping, bored and boring … until he comes to the jaguar. You'll be answering more Textual Analysis questions on the poem later, so be sure to ask your teacher if there's something you don't understand.

The Jaguar

The apes yawn and adore their fleas in the sun.
The parrots shriek as if they were on fire, or strut
Like cheap tarts to attract the stroller with the nut.
Fatigued with indolence, tiger and lion

5   Lie still as the sun. The boa-constrictor's coil
Is a fossil. Cage after cage seems empty, or
Stinks of sleepers from the breathing straw.
It might be painted on a nursery wall.

     But who runs like the rest past these arrives
10   At a cage where the crowd stands, stares, mesmerised,
As a child at a dream, at a jaguar hurrying enraged
Through prison darkness after the drills of his eyes

     On a short fierce fuse. Not in boredom –
The eye satisfied to be blind in fire,
15   By the bang of blood in the brain deaf the ear
He spins from the bars, but there's no cage to him

     More than to the visionary his cell:
His stride is wildernesses of freedom:
The world rolls under the long thrust of his heel.
20   Over the cage floor the horizons come.

Ted Hughes

Imagery: figures of speech using comparison

Simile

A simile is a figure of speech in which one thing is compared to another using the word *like* or the word *as*. This gives a more vivid picture because of the similarity between the two things compared.

For example:

'The parrots shriek **as if** they were on fire …'

This suggests the noise the parrots are making, which is so loud that it is as if they were in a fire. It might also suggest that the bright colours of the parrots, the red and orange, are like the bright colours of a fire.

Later in the poem, still referring to the parrots, Hughes says they:

> '... strut
> **Like** cheap tarts to attract the stroller with the nut.'

NOW TRY THIS

What image does this suggest in your mind about the way the parrots walk? Write your own sentence(s) starting with these words:

The simile 'strut like cheap tarts to attract the stroller with the nut' suggests...

(Indeed, even the **position** of the word '*strut*' at the end of the line is important. If a word is **deliberately** placed at the beginning or end of a line of poetry, it makes it stand out even more. This has to do with the poem's **structure**, which we will look at elsewhere.)

Metaphor

A metaphor is another figure of speech in which one thing is compared to another because of some point(s) of comparison between them. This time the words *like* and *as if* are **not** used. Instead one thing is said to **be** another thing.

For example:

'The boa-constrictor's coil is a fossil.'

A boa-constrictor is a snake that coils itself up in a spiral shape. A fossil is the imprint in stone of a creature that has been dead for millions of years. A very common type of fossil is the ammonite, the fossil of a shellfish which had a coiled, spiral shape.

Can you see what Ted Hughes is suggesting here? He is comparing the shape of the snake to the shape of an ammonite fossil, but he's also suggesting that the snake is so still it looks **as if** it has been lying there for millions of years.

Did you notice we had to use *as if* to help explain the metaphor? This shows how alike similes and metaphors are, but similes are easy to spot and metaphors are much more difficult. They do not always use the word *is*. Sometimes we have to ask ourselves if what the writer is saying can be literally true.

Look at the last three lines of the poem.

'His stride is wildernesses of freedom:
The world rolls under the long thrust of his heel.
Over the cage floor the horizons come.'

Each one of these lines is a metaphor.

Personification

Personification can be thought of as a special kind of metaphor. In **person**ification, an inanimate, non-living object is written about as if it was a **person** or a living creature. For example:

'Cage after cage ... stinks of sleepers from the breathing straw.'

Can straw breathe? Of course not – it is not a living creature. Ted Hughes is suggesting the straw **seems** alive because of the smell and breathing of the creatures hidden in it.

Figures of speech that involve sound

Onomatopoeia

When a word **sounds** like what it is describing, we call this **onomatopoeia**. For example:

'The apes **yawn** ...'

Or

'The parrots **shriek** ...'

Onomatopoeia is used to make the writing sound more realistic and dramatic. *Yawn* makes the reader slow down because of the long vowel sounds, and the way you have to open your mouth wide just to say it. You might be yawning by now, just hearing the word! In the poem it suggests the tiredness or boredom of the animals in the zoo.

NOW TRY THIS

How does *shriek* suggest the sound the parrots are making? Write your own sentence(s) starting:

The word 'shriek' suggests . . .

Alliteration

When letters or sounds are repeated, usually at the beginnings of words, we call this **alliteration**. For example:

'By the bang of blood in the brain ...'

Sometimes alliteration acts like a tongue-twister, and forces you to slow down to pronounce the words properly. This makes you notice them more and draws your attention to what the writer is saying. Here, all the stressed words begin with **b** and suggest one of those pounding headaches it's so difficult to get rid of.

NOW TRY THIS

Look at this line from the poem:

'stinks of sleepers from the breathing straw.'

What effect does the alliteration in this line have? What does it make you think of? Write your own sentence starting:

The alliteration in 'stinks of sleepers from the breathing straw' suggests...

As well as these two figures of speech, there are other language techniques connected with sound.

Other language techniques that involve sound

Repetition

One example of repetition in this poem is:

'**Cage** after **cage** ...'

This also slows down the reader, making us pay more attention to the repeated words. Here, it suggests endless cages with bored sleepy animals in them.

Long vowels

Long vowels say the names of the letters — ā, ē, ī, ō, ū, as in gāme, scēne, tīle, hōme, fūme. They can be marked by a long dash above the vowel. For example:

'The āpes yāwn and adōre their flēas ...'

If a line has a lot of long vowels this slows you down and draws your attention. Here it reflects the slowness, laziness and boredom of the animals in the zoo.

NOW TRY THIS

How does the **sound** of the expression 'fatigued with indolence' reflect the poet's meaning at this point? Write your own sentence(s) starting:

The expression 'fatigued with indolence' sounds . . .

Short vowels

Short vowels say the short sound of the letters – **a**, **e**, **i**, **o**, **u**, as in *pat*, *pet*, *pit*, *pot*, *cŭp*. They can be marked by a short cŭp sign above the vowel.

For example:

'Bŭt who rŭns like thĕ rĕst păst these ...'

If a line has a lot of short vowels, suggesting light and quick movement, they make you sit up and pay attention. Here the short vowels indicate a change of pace which lets you know something different is going to happen when the visitors move on and see the jaguar.

Hard consonants

Hard consonant sounds like **p**, **t**, **k** make the line sound sharp and hard. For example:

'The **parrots shriek** ... or **strut like cheap tarts** ...'

Hard consonants need to be pronounced carefully. They make you say each word separately and draw attention to the words, emphasising the raucous noise and obvious showing-off of the parrots.

Soft consonants

Soft consonant sounds like **b**, **d**, **n**, **m**, **s**, **l**, **r** make the poem sound softer and gentler. For example:

'**Fatigued** with **indolence**, tiger and **lion**
Lie still as the **sun**.'

Soft consonants are easier to run together. They can imitate a murmuring sound, or make the poem sound sleepy, reflecting the laziness and boredom of the animals in the zoo.

These language techniques are not in the poem by accident – all of them are there because of the careful word choice and skill of Ted Hughes.

NOW TRY THIS

Here are some Textual Analysis questions on the poem. Use the advice so far on language techniques, and the sentences you have written, to help you to answer them. Use your common sense too. Often Textual Analysis questions are not about specific language techniques that we can give a name to, but about common sense answers. Trust your judgement! Pay attention also to the marks allocated to each question. For 1 mark you probably just have to write one straightforward answer. For 2 marks you should answer in more detail, making two points, and so on.

The Jaguar

The apes yawn and adore their fleas in the sun.
The parrots shriek as if they were on fire, or strut
Like cheap tarts to attract the stroller with the nut.
Fatigued with indolence, tiger and lion

5   Lie still as the sun. The boa-constrictor's coil
Is a fossil. Cage after cage seems empty, or
Stinks of sleepers from the breathing straw.
It might be painted on a nursery wall.

But who runs like the rest past these arrives
10   At a cage where the crowd stands, stares, mesmerised,
As a child at a dream, at a jaguar hurrying enraged
Through prison darkness after the drills of his eyes

On a short fierce fuse. Not in boredom –
The eye satisfied to be blind in fire,
15   By the bang of blood in the brain deaf the ear
He spins from the bars, but there's no cage to him

More than to the visionary his cell:
His stride is wildernesses of freedom:
The world rolls under the long thrust of his heel.
20   Over the cage floor the horizons come.

Ted Hughes

The Jaguar – Textual Analysis questions

1. Comment on the **choice** of the word *adore* in the first line. What does this word suggest about the behaviour of the apes? **2**

2. How does the **simile** in line 2 help to give you a dramatic picture of the parrots? **2**

3. Identify the **figure of speech** in line 3, and say what it suggests to you about the parrots. **2**

4. Find another example of this **figure of speech** in the first two verses, and say what picture or image it suggests to you. **2**

5. Identify the **figure of speech** in 'The boa constrictor's coil is a fossil', and say what picture or image is suggested by it. **2**

6. Choose a word or expression from the first two stanzas (verses) which seems to make a good **sound effect**. How does it help you to get a strong impression of any of the animals or birds? Now do this question again for two more words or expressions from the first two verses, which help you to get a strong impression of any of the animals or birds. **6**

7. What do most of the zoo animals mentioned in the first two verses have in common? **1**

8. How does the poet make the speed of the poem change at the beginning of the third verse? **2**

9. How does the poet show by his **word choice** that the jaguar mentioned in the last three verses is very different from the animals in the first two verses? **2**

10. '*By the bang of blood in the brain deaf the ear*' (line 15): identify any **language technique** used here and say what effect it has in letting you know how the jaguar feels. **2**

11. Choose any two of the last three lines of the poem. Say what the line suggests to you, and say how effective the poet has been in suggesting this picture. **4**

12. What impression does Ted Hughes give of his feelings about the jaguar? **2**

13. What are *your* feelings about the jaguar? Give evidence from the poem to back up your answer. **1**

TOTAL 30 marks

You are about to see another poem. You may have read it already in English or History. It was written by Wilfred Owen, a young officer who died during the last few days of the First World War. Although he was brave and patriotic, he disapproved of the way the government was sending out young men to almost certain death – a bloody and horrible death, as you will see in the poem.

Don't be put off by the Latin title. '*Dulce et Decorum est pro patria mori*' means something like: 'It is sweet and noble to die for one's native land'. Owen is using the quotation ironically. He does *not* believe it is sweet and noble to die like this. In fact at the end of the poem he calls it a '*Lie*'.

Although this poem has very different subject matter from *The Jaguar*, Wilfred Owen uses a lot of the same language techniques as Ted Hughes.

NOW TRY THIS

Read the poem, and the answer the questions that follow.

Dulce et Decorum Est

Bent double, like old beggars under sacks,
Knock-kneed, coughing like hags, we cursed through sludge,
Till on the haunting flares we turned our backs
And towards our distant rest began to trudge.
5   Men marched asleep. Many had lost their boots
But limped on, blood-shod. All went lame; all blind;
Drunk with fatigue; deaf even to the hoots
Of tired, outstripped Five-Nines that dropped behind.

Gas! GAS! Quick, boys! – An ecstasy of fumbling,
10   Fitting the clumsy helmets just in time;
But someone still was yelling out and stumbling
And flound'ring like a man in fire or lime…
Dim, through the misty panes and thick green light,
As under a green sea, I saw him drowning.

15   In all my dreams, before my helpless sight,
He plunges at me, guttering, choking, drowning.

If in some smothering dreams you too could pace
Behind the wagon that we flung him in,
And watch the white eyes writhing in his face,
20   His hanging face, like a devil's sick of sin;
If you could hear, at every jolt, the blood
Come gargling from the froth-corrupted lungs,
Obscene as cancer, bitter as the cud
Of vile, incurable sores on innocent tongues, –
25   My friend, you would not tell with such high zest
To children ardent for some desperate glory,
The old Lie: Dulce et decorum est
Pro patria mori.

Wilfred Owen

Dulce et Decorum Est – Textual Analysis questions

1. Quote and show how effective the **simile** in the first line is in describing the soldiers. **2**

2. Quote another **comparison** in line 2, and show how it adds to the description of the soldiers. **2**

3. Choose a word or expression from line 2 which uses a **sound effect** to emphasise these pictures and say how it helps to do this. **2**

4. Why is *'Men marched asleep.'* (line 5) an important sentence in showing us what state they were in? You should identify and comment on two different **language techniques**. **4**

5. Comment on the effect of the unusual **word choice** in *'blood-shod'* in line 6. **2**

6. Choose an example of sound effects being used well in lines 6–7. Say what impression the sound effect makes. Now choose another example of a sound effect being used well in lines 6–7, and say what impression the sound effect makes. **4**

7. Show how any two **language techniques** used in *'Gas! GAS! Quick, boys!'* (line 9) make the poem exciting at this point. **4**

8. Quote a **simile** from verse 2 (lines 9–14) and show how it increases your horror at what is happening to the soldier. **2**

9. What is the effect of the build-up of the . .*ing* words in lines 9–16? – *'fumbling ... yelling ... stumbling ... flound'ring ... drowning ... guttering ... choking ... drowning.'* **2**

10. Quote the **comparison** in line 20 and say what effect it has on you. **2**

11. Choose any other **comparison** from lines 21–24 and show how it adds to your impression of his physical injuries. **2**

12. What is the main point that Wilfred Owen is making in this poem when he finishes with: *'The old Lie : Dulce et decorum est pro Patria mori.'* (It is sweet and noble to die for one's native land.)? Do you agree with him? Justify (give a reason for) your answer. **2**

TOTAL 30 marks

We've studied these poems to help you pass the Textual Analysis NAB, and to prepare you for analysis questions in the future. But, if you really like one of these poems, you can also write an essay about it in the Critical Essay section of the final exam in May. You will learn more about this in Chapter 9.

Textual Analysis NABs can also be based on extracts from novels, short stories or plays. In the following extract the writer, Robert Swindells, is writing from the point of view of a homeless teenager, Link. Swindells uses careful word choice and structure, and figures of speech such as simile and metaphor.

NOW TRY THIS

Read the passage carefully, and answer the questions as you did with the poems.

Stone Cold – Extract 1

The last days of January were a swine. I nearly went back to Vince. I mean it. It snowed every day so the pavements were thick with slush, and nothing gets inside a pair of trainers like slush can. Ginger

5 and I lurked in subways and doorways as much as we could but our feet were constantly wet and freezing just the same. Night after night, frost turned the slush to grey iron and crept into our damp bedding to stiffen footwear and make sleep

10 impossible. And if you think it's bound to make the punters more generous with their change, seeing kids wet and shivering, forget it. It had the opposite effect. Everybody slogged grimly by and their hands never left their pockets unless they

15 were wearing gloves. Nobody stopped. Maybe they thought they'd die if they stopped, like explorers at the South Pole.

We grew hungry. Really hungry. The cold seems to settle in your bones when there's nothing in your

20 stomach. You can't shift it. We tried everything – stamping our feet, running on the spot, blowing into our hands, huddling together in the subway. It was no use. All we could do was keep moving through sleepless nights and days that merged into

25 one another till we no longer knew what day it was or whether it was morning or evening. One time, Ginger borrowed a marker pen from an old newsvendor and printed a couple of placards which read, NON-ALCOHOLIC HOMELESS, PLEASE HELP. He

30 said you had to put non-alcoholic because people seldom give to winos. We sat in a subway somewhere with our feet and legs in our sleeping-bags and the placards on the muddy tiles, but he might as well have put EVIL, SHIFTLESS BABY-

35 KICKER, AFTER YOUR DOSH for all the good it did us.

Robert Swindells

Stone Cold – Extract 1: Textual Analysis questions

1. The **word choice** in paragraph 1 makes you feel sorry for Link and Ginger. Quote two expressions and show how each one makes you feel sorry for the homeless boys. **2**

2. *'Night after night, frost turned the slush to grey iron and crept into our damp bedding to stiffen footwear and make sleep impossible.'* (lines 7–10). Pick out a **comparison** from this sentence, and show how it makes you feel sorry for the homeless boys. **2**

3. Quote a **simile** from the last sentences of the first paragraph and show how this simile is a good one to use here. **2**

4. *'We tried everything – stamping our feet, running on the spot, blowing into our hands, huddling together in the subway.'* (lines 20–22). How does the **structure** of this **sentence** help you to get a clear picture of their situation? **2**

5. How does the **contrast** in the **word choice** between the placards: *'NON ALCOHOLIC, HOMELESS, PLEASE HELP'* and *'EVIL, SHIFTLESS BABYKICKER, AFTER YOUR DOSH'* help you to see how hopeless their begging was? **2**

Sentence structure questions

Question 4 above was a question about **sentence structure**. Often questions just ask you to *comment on the sentence structure*, and you may be left wondering where to start.

In the example above there are a number of features of **punctuation** which help to give you clues on how to answer. Because punctuation is a used by writers to help structure their sentences, it follows that looking at the punctuation can often help you to answer sentence structure questions. In question 4 above, we have:

■ three short words introducing the sentence before a **dash** to introduce a longer explanation of what the 'everything' was that they did to keep warm

■ a **dash** to introduce a **list** of how many things they did to try to keep themselves warm

■ **commas** separating the items in the list to make them clearer and to show what each thing was that they tried.

As well as looking at the punctuation, there are also a few questions to ask yourself when you come across sentence structure questions:

- Is the sentence short? Is it very long? What effect does this length have?

- Is the sentence in the form of a question? Or exclamation! What effect does this have?

- Is the sentence in the form of a list? What effect does this have?

- Have the words been placed in an unusual order? What effect does this have?

- Is there anything else unusual about the way the sentence is written?

Conversational tone

You are about to see another extract from *Stone Cold* in which Robert Swindells has the homeless teenager, Link, describe the problems of sleeping rough. He writes this in a very **conversational tone**, as if Link was talking directly to us. Link uses *you* throughout, for example in '*If you think* …'. He also uses shortened forms such as *it's, won't, doesn't*, which are also **markers** of a conversational tone. They are the kind of things people say when they are speaking to you.

NOW TRY THIS

Read the extract and answer the questions. Look out for **tone** and **sentence structure** questions.

Stone Cold – Extract 2

If you think sleeping rough's just a matter of finding a dry spot where the fuzz won't move you on and getting your head down, you're wrong. Not your fault of course – if you've never tried it you've no way of knowing what it's like, so what I thought I'd do was sort of talk you through a typical night. That night in the Vaudeville alcove
5   won't do, because there were two of us and it's worse if you're by yourself.

So you pick your spot. Wherever it is (unless you're in a squat or a derelict house or something) it's going to have a floor of stone, tile, concrete or brick. In other words it's going to be hard and cold. It might be a bit cramped, too – shop doorways often are. And remember, if it's winter you're going to be half frozen
10 before you even start. Anyway you've got your place, and if you're lucky enough to have a sleeping-bag you unroll it and get in.

Settled for the night? Well maybe, maybe not. Remember my first night? The Scouser? 'Course you do. He kicked me out of my bedroom and pinched my watch. Well, that sort of thing can happen any night, and there are worse things. You

15 could be peed on by a drunk or a dog. Happens all the time – one man's bedroom is another man's lavatory. You might be spotted by a gang of lager louts on the look-out for someone to maim. That happens all the time too, and if they get carried away you can end up dead. There are the guys who like young boys, who think because you're a dosser you'll do anything for dosh, and there's the psycho

20 who'll knife you for your pack.

So, you lie listening. You bet you do. Footsteps. Voices. Breathing, even. Doesn't help you sleep.

Then there's your bruises. What bruises? Try lying on a stone floor for half an hour. Just half an hour. You can choose any position you fancy, and you can change

25 position as often as you like. You won't find it comfy, I can tell you. You won't sleep unless you're dead drunk or zonked on downers. And if you are, and do, you're going to wake up with bruises on hips, shoulders, elbows, ankles and knees – especially if you're a bit thin from not eating properly. And if you do that six hours a night for six nights you'll feel like you fell out of a train. Try sleeping on concrete then.

30 And don't forget the cold. If you've ever tried dropping off to sleep with cold feet, even in bed, you'll know it's impossible. You've got to warm up those feet, or lie awake. And in January, in a doorway, in wet trainers, it can be quite a struggle. And if you manage it, chances are you'll need to get up for a pee, and then it starts all over again.

35 And those are only some of the hassles. I haven't mentioned stomach cramps from hunger, headaches from the flu, toothache, fleas and lice. I haven't talked about homesickness, depression or despair. I haven't gone into how it feels to want a girl-friend when your circumstances make it virtually impossible for you to get one – how it feels to know you're a social outcast in fact, a non-person to whom every

40 ordinary everyday activity is closed.

So. You lie on your bruises, listening. Trying to warm your feet. You curl up on your side and your hip hurts, so you stretch out on your back so your feet stay cold and the concrete hurts your heels. You force yourself to lie still for a bit, thinking that'll help you drop off, but it doesn't. Your pack feels like a rock under your head and

45 your nose is cold. You wonder what time it is. Can you stop listening now, or could someone still come? Distant chimes. You strain your ears, counting. One o'clock? It can't be only one o'clock, surely? I've been here hours. Did I miss a chime?

What's that? Sounds like breathing. Heavy breathing, as in maniac. Lie still. Quiet. Maybe he won't see you. Listen. Is he still there? Silence now. Creeping up,

50 perhaps. No. Relax. Jeez, my feet are cold.

Robert Swindells

Stone Cold – Extract 2: Textual Analysis questions

1. The passage is written in a **conversational tone**, as if Link was speaking directly to the reader. Give two examples of a conversational tone from the first paragraph.   2

2. How does the **sentence structure** in lines 12 and 13 give the impression that Link is talking to you?   2

3. How does the **sentence structure** in lines 21 and 22 help you to understand what Link was feeling at that moment?   2

4. How does the **sentence structure** in lines 45–47 make an impact on you?   2

5. Comment on the effectiveness of the last paragraph as an ending to the whole passage.   2

NOW TRY THIS

We are going to try a full-length Textual Analysis paper from the same novel by Robert Swindells. This time he adopts the persona (writes from the point of view) of a former soldier who has become a psychopathic serial killer, targeting homeless people.

Stone Cold – Extract 3

Time for a brief discourse on the subject of killing. Killing humans. Murder, not to put too fine a point on it.

Oh yes, that's what they'd call it. If they ever found out about it, which they won't. Murder. The deliberate killing by a human being of another human being. But you
5   see, I was trained to kill. As a soldier, it was my chief function to kill, waste, do in – whatever you want to call it – those among my fellow humans whose activities happened to displease the powers that be in my country. And this is where the confusion arises. This is where distinctions get a bit blurred. The killing by a soldier of the enemies of his country is not murder. They don't jail you for it. In fact, if you
10 do it really well they give you a medal. So why, if I'm disposing of these druggy dossers whose activities are dragging the country down, am I a murderer? It's all nonsense. I'm not a murderer at all – I'm a soldier out of uniform, killing for his country. Trouble is, is that because the country doesn't approve, the whole thing

15 becomes a hole-and-corner affair. You've got to hide what you're doing, and that
brings us to the hard part, which is DISPOSING OF THE BODY.

You see, soldiers – soldiers in uniform – don't have this problem. They don't have
to conceal the bodies of their victims. Quite the reverse in fact. They lay 'em out in
rows, count 'em, take snapshots of 'em, like shooting parties used to do with
pheasant. Only difference is they don't eat 'em. They shove 'em in a big hole and
20 bury 'em and that's that. No problem. Everyone knows they're there, nobody cares.
But if you're out of uniform, like me – if you're what they call a murderer – you've
got to get rid of the body, and that's a real worry because, believe it or not, it's far
and away the hardest bit of the whole job.

Killing's easy. Dead easy. Especially if you've been trained to it, though of course
25 anyone can do it if they put their mind to it, but more murderers have come
unstuck because they made a mess of disposing of the body than through any
other cause. It's a fact.

Everything's been tried. Acid baths. Dismemberment. Cement boots and a deep
river. Everything. And more often than not it's no use – the body (or parts of it)
30 turns up sooner or later and the killer is caught.

I won't be. No. Because unlike most so-called murderers, I've planned in advance.
My flat's on the ground floor, and there's a handy little space – quite a big space,
actually – under the floorboards. It's beautifully ventilated – stick your hand down
there and you feel the draught – so it'll stay cool, even on the warmest day. That's
35 important. I won't go into why because it's not a pleasant subject – let's just say
bodies in a warm place have a way of betraying their presence after a day or two.
So – I've got this place – like to think of it as my built-in refrigerator – and that's
where our little friend of last night now lies. As I have said, he doesn't feel the
cold, nor is he cluttering up anyone's doorway. The whole thing's so much tidier,
40 don't you think?

Robert Swindells

Stone Cold – Extract 3: Textual Analysis questions

1. What is the effect of the writer's **repetition** of words and ideas in '*... killing.   Killing humans. Murder ...*' (lines 1–2)? **2**

2. How do the short sentences in the first paragraph (lines 1–2) make the ideas more dramatic? **2**

3. Look again at the following from the second paragraph (line 4): '*Murder. The deliberate killing by a human being of another human being.*' What is the writer doing in these two sentences? Copy and complete:

   a) In the first sentence he_____
   b) In the second sentence he_____
   c) How effective do you find this technique? **3**

4. '*... it was my chief function to <u>kill, waste, do in ...</u>*' (line 5)

   a) What is **the same** about the underlined words?
   b) What is **different** about the underlined words?
   c) What is the effect of this listing of words? **3**

5. The writer frequently has the character repeat words and ideas.

   Find another expression in the second paragraph (lines 3–15) which means roughly the same as '*This is where distinctions get a bit blurred.*' (line 8). What effect does this have? **2**

6. '*So why, if I'm disposing of these druggy dossers whose activities are dragging the country down, am I a murderer?*' (lines 10–11)

   a) How does the **word choice** in this sentence show what the speaker's attitude is to the homeless? **2**
   b) How does the **sentence structure** in this sentence involve you in his thinking? **2**

7. Why do you think '*DISPOSING OF THE BODY*' (line 15) is printed in capital letters? What effect does this have? **2**

8. According to this paragraph (lines 3–15), what is the most difficult thing about murder? How does the writer emphasise this? **2**

9. '*They lay 'em out in rows, count 'em, take snapshots of 'em like shooting parties used to do with pheasant.*' (lines 17–19)

   a) How does the **word choice** in this sentence show what the speaker's attitude is to dead bodies? **2**
   b) How does the **sentence structure** in this sentence add to the same attitude? **2**

10. How does the **sentence structure** in lines 28–30 give a shocking impression? **2**

11. One of the features of the **punctuation** of this passage is the way pairs of dashes are used to mark off an extra piece of information in the middle of a sentence. For example: '*My flat's on the ground floor, and there's a handy little space – quite a big*

space, actually – under the floorboards.' (lines 32–33).

Quote another sentence from this paragraph, or from earlier in the passage, where a pair of dashes is used to mark off an extra piece of information.

What effect does this have?   2

12. The passage finishes with *'The whole thing's so much tidier, don't you think?'* This suggests a very conversational **tone** or style.

Find two more markers of a conversational tone from anywhere in this passage.   2

TOTAL 30 marks

NOW TRY THIS

Here is an extract from a novel called *Hoot* by an American writer, Carl Hiaasen. In this extract the main character Roy sees a strange running boy. Roy is being bullied by a boy called Dana Matherson because he is new to the area. Read the extract and answer the questions.

Hoot

Roy would not have noticed the strange boy if it weren't for Dana Matherson, because Roy ordinarily didn't look out the window of the school bus. He preferred to read comics and mystery books on the morning ride to Trace Middle.

5   But on this day, a Monday (Roy would never forget), Dana Matherson grabbed Roy's head from behind and pressed his thumbs into Roy's temple, as if he were squeezing a soccer ball. The older kids were supposed to stay in the back of the bus, but Dana had snuck up behind Roy's seat and ambushed him. When Roy tried to wriggle free, Dana mushed his face against the window.

It was then, squinting through the smudged glass, that Roy spotted the strange boy
10   running along the sidewalk. It appeared as if he was hurrying to catch the school bus, which had stopped at a corner to pick up more kids.

The boy was straw-blond and wiry, and his skin was nut-brown from the sun. The expression on his face was intent and serious. He wore a faded Miami Heat basketball jersey and dirty khaki shorts, and here was the odd part: no shoes. The
15   soles of his bare feet looked as black as barbecue coals.

Trace Middle school didn't have the world's strictest dress code, but Roy was pretty sure that some sort of footwear was required. The boy might have been carrying sneakers in his backpack, if only he'd been wearing a backpack. No shoes, no backpack, no books – strange, indeed, on a school day.

20 Roy was sure that the barefoot boy would catch all kinds of grief from Dana and the other big kids once he boarded the bus, but that didn't happen...

Because the boy kept running – past the corner, past the line of students waiting to get on the bus; past the bus itself. Roy wanted to shout, 'Hey look at that guy!' but his mouth wasn't working so well. Dana Matherson still had him from behind,
25 pushing his face against the window.

As the bus pulled away from the intersection, Roy hoped to catch another glimpse of the boy further up the street. However, he had turned off the sidewalk and was now cutting across a private yard – running very fast, much faster than Roy could run and maybe even faster than Richard, Roy's best friend back in Montana. Richard
30 was so fast that he got to work out with the high school track squad when he was only in seventh grade.

Dana Matherson was digging his fingernails into Roy's scalp, trying to make him squeal, but Roy barely felt a thing. He was gripped with curiosity as the running boy dashed through one neat green yard after another, getting smaller in Roy's
35 vision as he put a wider distance between himself and the school bus.

Roy saw a big pointy-eared dog, probably a German shepherd, bound off somebody's porch and go for the boy. Incredibly, the boy didn't change his course. He vaulted over the dog, crashed through a cherry hedge, and then disappeared from view.

Carl Hiaasen

Hoot – Textual Analysis questions

1. What is the **setting** in time and place of this extract? (**Where** and **when** does the incident begin?) 2

2. Comment on the **choice of verbs** used in paragraph 2 (lines 4–8) to describe what Dana Matherson does to Roy. (Write down four separate doing words saying what Dana does to Roy. Say what impression these words give you of the way Dana treats Roy.) 2

3. Dana presses Roy's head 'as if he were squeezing a soccer ball.' (lines 5–6). Say what **figure of speech** this is, and what impression it gives you of the way Dana treats Roy. 2

4. Why does the writer say 'squinting through the smudged glass' (paragraph 3, line 9) rather than simply using the word looking? What does the

word *squinting* suggest, which is more detailed than just looking? **2**

5. The writer uses words with hyphens in them in paragraph 4 to describe the boy's hair and skin. Explain what is meant by '*straw-blond*' and '*nut-brown*' (line 12). Why are these good words to use here? **3**

6. What does the word '*wiry*' (line 12) suggest about the boy? **1**

7. Look again at paragraph 4 (lines 12–15). How does the writer's **punctuation** and **sentence structure** draw attention to the oddest thing about the boy? **2**

8. '*The soles of his bare feet looked as black as barbecue coals.*' (lines 14–15) The writer uses two separate **language techniques** in this sentence to describe the boy's bare feet. Pick out each one and say what the language technique is, and say what effect it has. **4**

9. '*No shoes, no backpack, no books – strange, indeed, on a school day.*' (lines 18–19)

The writer mentions three unusual things about the boy –

what **language techniques** does he use to draw attention to them? **3**

10. What is unusual about the connection between paragraphs 6 and 7? (lines 20–25) **2**

11. How does the writer emphasise the running of the boy in the first sentence of paragraph 7? (lines 22–23) **2**

12. The writer uses the same techniques in paragraph 8 (lines 26–31) as in paragraph 7. Use your answer to question 11 to help you to answer. How does the writer emphasise the **speed** of the boy running? Select a quotation from the paragraph, and comment on how well this shows his speed. **2**

13. Which single word used in the last paragraph (lines 36–38) emphasises how unusual it is that the boy was not bothered by the dog? **1**

14. Pick out two verbs used in the last sentence, and say how they show that the boy was determined to keep on running. **2**

TOTAL 30 marks

In one of the extracts we read from *Stone Cold*, Robert Swindells had to adopt the persona of (pretend to be) a psychopathic serial killer – not an easy thing for a completely sane person to do! In the following extract, the writer adopts the persona of a young man looking back on his childhood. The butterflies on the page indicate the change from young man to little boy. After the butterflies his word choice and sentence structure become much simpler, reflecting a little boy's point of view.

Private Peaceful

They've gone now, and I'm alone at last. I have the whole night ahead of me, and I won't waste a single moment of it. I shan't sleep it away. I won't dream it away either. I mustn't, because every moment of it will be far too precious.

5   I want to try to remember everything, just as it was, just as it happened. I've had nearly eighteen years of yesterdays and tomorrows, and tonight I must remember as many of them as I can. I want tonight to be long, as long as my life, not filled with fleeting dreams that rush me on towards dawn.

Tonight, more than any other night of my life, I want to feel alive.

Charlie is taking me by the hand, leading me because he knows I don't want to go.
10   I've never worn a collar before and it's choking me. My boots are strange and heavy on my feet. My heart is heavy too, because I dread what I am going to. Charlie has told me often how terrible this school-place is: about Mr Munnings and his raging tempers and the long whipping cane he hangs on the wall above his desk.

Big Joe doesn't have to go to school and I don't think that's fair at all. He's much
15   older than me. He's even older than Charlie and he's never been to school. He stays at home with Mother, and sits up in his tree singing *Oranges and Lemons*, and laughing. Big Joe is always happy, always laughing. I wish I could be happy like him. I wish I could be at home like him. I don't want to go with Charlie. I don't want to go to school.

20 I look back, over my shoulder, hoping for a reprieve, hoping that Mother will come running after me and take me home. But she doesn't come and she doesn't come, and school and Mr Munnings and his cane are getting closer with every step.

'Piggyback?' says Charlie. He sees my eyes full of tears and knows how it is. Charlie always knows how it is. He's three years older than me, so he's done everything
25 and knows everything. He's strong, too, and very good at piggybacks. So I hop up and cling on tight, crying behind my closed eyes, trying not to whimper out loud. But I cannot hold back my sobbing for long because I know that this morning is not the beginning of anything – not new and exciting as Mother says it is – but rather the end of my beginning. Clinging on round Charlie's neck I know that I am
30 living the last moments of my carefree time, that I will not be the same person when I come home this afternoon.

Michael Morpurgo

Private Peaceful – Textual Analysis questions

1. In the first paragraph, note the **repetition** of the words 'I won't …', 'I shan't …', 'I won't …', 'I mustn't …'. What impression do these words give of the young man's feelings about his situation? 2

2. Which expression in this paragraph shows his feelings about his childhood memories? Quote it, and say **how** it shows the strength of his feelings. 2

3. In the next two paragraphs before the butterflies, the writer uses a lot of **repetition**. Write down two examples of repetition and say what they tell us about the boy. 4

4. How does the writer make the last paragraph (line 8) of this section stand out? 2

5. Write down two details from the first paragraph after the butterflies (lines 9–13) which suggest that this story is set a long time ago. 2

6. Quote four separate words from this paragraph which show that the boy has a very negative impression of school. 2

7. What details are given in the paragraph about his brother Big Joe (lines 14–19) which suggest why Big Joe does not have to go to school? What do these suggest to you? 2

8. How do the last four sentences of this paragraph (lines 17–19) suggest a very child-like attitude? 2

9. 'I look back, over my shoulder …' (line 20). How can you tell from the way the rest of this paragraph is written that the boy **keeps on** looking back over his shoulder? 2

10. Look again at the last paragraph. How does the writer's **word choice** show the boy's admiration for his big brother Charlie?   2

11. Write down four separate words or expressions from the last paragraph which show how upset the little boy is.   2

12. Write down two expressions from the last paragraph which show that the little boy is trying to hide his feelings.   2

13. What other expression in this paragraph suggests the same idea as '*the end of my beginning*'?   2

14. Explain what the writer suggests by the mysterious last sentence '*I will not be the same person when I come home this afternoon.*'   2

TOTAL 30 marks

Your teacher will decide when you are ready to try a Textual Analysis NAB. When you pass this you will have completed a major part of the course. Remember too that all the analysis skills you have used in this chapter will be useful to you in the next chapter of this book as you practise Close Reading for that NAB and for the final SQA examination in the middle of May. Your analysis skills will also help you in your study of literature. You will find more advice about this in another part of this book.

2 Close Reading

Close Reading is a very important part of Intermediate English. You will have to pass a NAB in Close Reading in order to pass the course, but you will also have to sit a paper in Close Reading as part of the SQA examination. This makes up 50% of your final grade.

Close Reading passages at Intermediate level will always be non-fiction prose passages. In the past few years, these have been extracts from good newspaper articles, travel books and autobiographies, and non-fiction books on a variety of subjects. Close Reading exercises are always worth 30 marks. The passages used in this book have been shortened here. You might like to read them in full by finding the books that the extracts come from in your library.

You have already done Close Reading in 5–14 English or in Standard Grade, (where it was known simply as Reading). All the techniques you learned there will be useful, as will the techniques in the Textual Analysis section (Chapter 1) of this book.

Why do the examiners want to test you further in Close Reading? Well, for a start, they expect you to show you can read and understand more adult pieces of writing. Employers, colleges and universities want to know they have taken on a young person who has reached a certain adult standard in Close Reading. You are reading this book, so presumably you want to show your Close Reading abilities too!

They will ask questions of three different types:

- **Understanding** questions test how well you understand **what** the writer has written.

- **Analysis** questions test how well you can identify **how** the writer has written it.

- **Evaluation** tests you on **how well** the writer has written.

There will be a code letter (U, A, E) alongside each question to help you to know what type of answer is required.

If you are really serious about passing Intermediate, one of the best things you can do is *start reading more NOW!*

- If your family regularly reads a good newspaper like the *Scotsman*, *Herald*, *Guardian* or *Times*, start reading more articles from that. Perhaps you can discuss what you read with your parents or other adults – but don't take the paper away until they've finished it…!

- If you have access to the Internet, most good newspapers have websites where you can read and download interesting articles.

- Read more about your own favourite sport or pastime.
- Read a biography or autobiography of a famous person.

- Read travel books about the places you might visit when you have passed your exams.

- Read so that you can follow the argument in a piece of writing – that is, follow the writer's main line of thought. Sometimes putting these in bullet points helps.

- Read so that you understand the meaning of what the writer is saying – sometimes you can work out unfamiliar words from the context; at other times you may need a dictionary to check the meaning of a word or expression. But you will not have the use of a dictionary in the exam, so it's important to work on building up your vocabulary.

Understanding

Explain in your own words

Understanding questions ask you to show your understanding in a number of ways. Often questions start *Explain in your own words* ….You then have to use your own words to explain what is meant by a word or expression in the passage, or the main point the writer is making, or the reason for something that happens in the passage.

Here are some frequently asked **Understanding** questions:

- *Explain in your own words what is meant by _____ in line _____.*

- *Explain in your own words the three main points made by the writer in paragraph ____.*

- *Explain in your own words why...*

Context questions

Sometimes the question uses the word *context*. The question might ask you to *Work out from the context* … what is meant by a word or expression. **Context** means the words nearby in the sentence or paragraph. If the question asks you to work out from the context, there will always be clues to help you, for example words which mean the same kind of thing, examples, or explanations. Indeed we can even use a formula to answer these questions.

Here are some ways the examiners might ask context questions:

- *Explain in your own words what is meant by _____ in this context.*

- *How does the context of paragraph _____ help you to work out what is meant by _____?*

- *Work out from the context what is meant by _____ in paragraph _____.*

You are about to see an example of a **context** question, and a **formula** to help you answer it.

First, here is the short extract the question refers to:

> Vocational workers such as builders, electricians, cooks and hairdressers were more happy in their jobs than white-collar staff and felt more appreciated in their work.

Now here's the question:

How does the context of this paragraph help you to work out what is meant by 'vocational workers'?

As you can see, the phrase '*Vocational workers*' in the passage is followed by a list of examples '*such as builders, electricians, cooks and hairdressers …*'. These people all work practically and with their hands. This suggests that here, the writer is using '*vocational workers*' to mean people who do practical work with their hands. So how can we put this together in an answer?

Here is a possible answer:

The expression 'vocational workers' as used here means people who do practical work or work with their hands. I can work this out from the context because the expression is followed by a list of vocational workers: 'builders, electricians, cooks and hairdressers'. This gives the impression that vocational workers are people who work with their hands.

Context questions are usually worth 2 marks, and this answer would definitely get 2 marks because we have:

1. given a meaning for the expression *vocational workers*

2. quoted an extract from the paragraph, and explained how it helped us to work out the meaning.

If you follow this formula, you will always gain the full 2 marks for context questions.

Formula for context questions

We said earlier that there was a formula for context questions. If you learn the following words, you can use them every time you try this type of question.

> The expression '_____' as used here means
> _____. I can work this out from the context
> because it says '_____'. This
> suggests/means/gives the impression that
> _____.

However, fewer than half of the questions you have to answer in Close Reading are marked with the **U** that indicates an Understanding question. The others are marked with **A** for Analysis or **E** for Evaluation. You have already studied Analysis questions in Chapter 1, and indeed you have done a bit of Evaluation too, because that just indicates you have to say how well something has been expressed, or how effective it is. Looking at the letters – **U**, **A**, **E** – will help you to see how you are expected to answer the question.

NOW TRY THIS

The following newspaper article appeared in *The Scotsman* following a poll to see which workers were happiest in their jobs. Read the passage carefully, and then answer the questions, **using your own words** where asked to do so, and using the formula to help you answer the **context** questions. Note that the same word can mean different things in different contexts!

Hairdressers a Cut Above in the World of Happiness at Work

When it combs to happiness at work, it seems that fun-loving hairdressers have a head start

HAIRDRESSERS are the happiest employees while social workers and architects are the most
5   miserable professionals, according to a new survey.

Nearly half of the hairdressers said they always genuinely enjoyed their job, whereas just 2 per cent of social workers and architects said they were happy to turn up to
10 work every day. Next in the league of career contentment after crimpers were members of the clergy, chefs, beauticians and plumbers.

The poll of 1,200 employees by the qualifications body City and Guilds showed that workers are happier now than a year ago.

Vocational workers such as builders, electricians, cooks and hairdressers were more
15 happy in their jobs than white-collar staff and felt more appreciated in their work.

Tradesmen and women also had a better social life at work than white-collar employees such as accountants, bankers, estate agents or scientists.

Chris Humphries, the Director General of City and Guilds, said workers were now attaching increasing importance to happiness because jobs were taking up more
20 hours.

He said, 'Nowadays true job satisfaction and happiness is about fulfilling your full potential, tapping into your own creativity and feeling that you can make a difference.

'More people than ever are swapping their desk-bound jobs for a vocation that enables them to be hands-on, use their brains and be in charge of their own destiny.
25 As we spend so much time at work, it's important that we enjoy what we do and build on the skills that we are good at.'

Dr Cynthia McVey, a psychologist at Glasgow Caledonian University, added: 'Blue-collar workers like plumbers get the daily satisfaction of going home having seen a practical

job well done, like the installation of a boiler. White-collar workers are part of a chain
30 and often don't see results of their labour and so are more prone to stress.'

Charles Kivlin, 56, who runs a hair salon in Edinburgh's New Town, said his staff were
happy because being friendly and chatty to customers was a key part of their job. The
hairdresser even sends his staff to motivational classes to ensure they are content at
work.

35 He said: 'Another reason hairdressers are happy is because it is a popular profession
for young people to break into.

'They tend to be passionate about it and realise they can have great fun at work.
When people get their hair cut, they expect staff to be chirpy, so it gives my staff a
licence to enjoy themselves. Our motto here is make money first but also have fun.
40 Even though I have been in this job for over three decades, I still really enjoy my
personal ordinary day in the office.'

Edward Black, *The Scotsman*

Hairdressers … – Close Reading questions

Remember: the letters U, A, E will help you to answer the questions.

1. Re-read the first two paragraphs. Starting with hairdressers and working down, put the seven groups of employees mentioned in order of the happiness they feel at work. **4 U**

2. *'Next in the league of career contentment after crimpers'* (line 10)

   a) What does the word 'crimpers' mean here? How can you work that out from the **context**? **2 U**
   b) How does the word 'crimpers' create a humorous **tone**? **2 A**

c) Why is the word 'league' a good one to use in this paragraph? **2 A**

3. How does the writer **structure** his **sentences** in lines 8–17 so that he can pack in the maximum amount of information? **2 A**

4. Look at lines 12–13. Apart from showing which groups of workers were the happiest, what else did this poll show? **2 U**

5. How does the **context** of paragraph 4 (lines 14–15) help you to work out what is meant by 'vocational' here? **2 U**

6. How does the **context** of paragraphs 4 and 5 (lines 14–17) help you to work out what is meant by 'white-collar' workers here? **2 U**

7. Explain **in your own words** why, according to Chris Humphries in lines 18–20, workers are now attaching increasing importance to happiness in the workplace. **2 U**

8. Read lines 21–22. What is **one** of the main factors in '*true job satisfaction and happiness*'? Answer **in your own words**. **2 U**

9. What is meant by '*vocation*' in the **context** of lines 23–26? **2 U**

10. Explain **in your own words** why the '*blue collar*' and '*white collar*' workers referred to in lines 27–30 have different levels of job satisfaction at work. **2 U**

11. Charles Kivlin, interviewed in lines 35–41, talks about his work and his staff. Quote and comment on two examples to show how the **word choice** used here creates a light-hearted **tone**. **2 A**

12. Explain the double meanings in the **headline** and **sub-heading**. How are they effective in establishing the light-hearted **tone** of this article? **2 E**

TOTAL – 30 marks

Using your own words

Questions 7, 8 and 10 above asked you to answer **in your own words**. That is one of ways the SQA can find out whether you have understood an extract from the passage. If you can put it in your own words, it shows you have understood it. Occasionally you will understand something, but find it quite difficult to put the extract into your own words. Sometimes it seems there **is** only one way of saying it, at other times the words or ideas may be quite difficult. The SQA sometimes recognise this by asking you to answer **in your own words as far as possible**. You should try really hard to do this, or you may lose the marks that could make the difference between a Pass and a Fail or between an A and a B.

If you can't think of other words for your answer, trying putting the expression from the passage in a different order. Sometimes that is enough to give you good ideas for some other words. At least you won't have written down exactly what was in the passage, which would mean no marks.

Let's look at an example of putting expressions **in your own words**. Read this extract from a magazine article about Arthur's Seat, one of Edinburgh's extinct volcanoes.

Arthur's Seat

This Edinburgh volcano erupted under water before becoming inactive some 325 million years ago. Geologically, what remains is a basalt lava plug which choked the neck before being gradually buried along with the ash cone under thousands of feet of sediment.

Now look at the question:

> **Using your own words as far as possible,** write down two stages in the geological development of Arthur's Seat from the first paragraph.   2   U

The SQA are quite happy for you to use bullet points in some of your Close Reading answers. You could write something like:

- *The volcano exploded under water.*

- *Lava plugged the mouth of the volcano.*

- *Sediment covered it all.*

Any two of these three bullet points would do because the question only asks for two.

There's not much we can do about technical words such as 'volcano', 'lava', or 'sediment'. But you can say *exploded* instead of 'erupted', you could talk about the *mouth* of the volcano instead of its 'neck', and you could say it was *covered by sediment* instead of 'gradually buried'.

You can also take an expression like '*basalt lava plug which choked the neck*' and change it to '*lava plugged the mouth*', changing the noun *plug* to the verb *plugged*.

Another technique is to change the order of expressions so that instead of saying '*before being gradually buried along with the ash cone under thousands of feet of sediment*', you start with *sediment*, and simplify it to '*sediment covered it all.*'

We've used four useful techniques here:

1. Changing words (for example *erupted* to *exploded*)

2. Changing parts of speech (for example *plug* to *plugged*)

3. Changing the order of words (for example putting *sediment* at the beginning)

4. Simplify!

NOW TRY THIS

Do exactly the same with the example below.

First here's the passage:

> Movements in the earth's crust eventually caused folding, leaving the volcano tilted at an angle of 25 degrees. Its upper slopes were then worn away by glaciation and the weather, leaving one of the most accessible rock cliffs anywhere of an ancient volcano.
>
> *Instant* magazine

Now answer the question below:

> Using your own words as far as possible, write down another two stages in the development of Arthur's Seat from the second paragraph.   2   U

Following the argument/line of thought

One of the most important things you need to be able to do in the Close Reading NAB and final exam is **follow the argument**. This is really important for your future life and work too – employers need to know that you can understand what a piece of writing is about, and make appropriate decisions on it.

Follow the argument here just means **understand the line of thought** in the writing. We are not talking about a '*No I didn't/Yes you did*' type of argument! Following the argument involves more than just understanding the words. You need to be able to think about the words and understand the thoughts behind them, and their **implications** – what they imply, or suggest, but may not actually say outright.

NOW TRY THIS

The following extract is from a newspaper article about the way parents speak to their children in two different types of families. Read the passage carefully and then answer all the questions, using your own words where asked to do so.

Chattering Classes

American academics Betty Hart and Todd Risley carried out an astonishing piece of research between 1995 and 1998. For two-and-a-half years they studied 42 families with toddlers, recording what was said to the children.

5   Their data, which took six years to analyse, showed that professional parents spoke almost 1,500 words more every hour than unemployed parents. Thus a child in a professional family heard 11 million words a year, while a child growing up on benefit heard just 3 million.

Hart and Risley also analysed the type of language used and found that children from professional families received 700,000 words of encouragement, with just 80,000
10 negatives. The child from the family on benefit heard 60,000 words of encouragement and 120,000 negatives. The Hart-Risley research appears to confirm, again, the damage that deprivation can do to a child.

Times Educational Supplement

Chattering Classes – Close Reading questions

1. What does the word 'astonishing' (line 1) suggest about the results of this research? **1 U**

Look again at lines 4–7.

2. Who were the two groups of parents studied? **2 U**

3. Write down, in your own words as far as possible, the first astonishing fact the researchers discovered. **2 U**

Look again at lines 8–12.

4. Which word indicates that they did further research? **1 U**

5. In your own words as far as possible, write down the next astonishing fact they discovered. **2 U**

6. Again, as far as possible in your own words, write down the overall result that Hart and Risley have discovered from this research. **2 U**

TOTAL – 10 marks

What are the **implications** of this piece of research? You could say that parents who want their children to do well should **talk** to their children as much as possible, using as much **positive** language as possible – for example *Well done! Good boy!*

Using linking words

Writers often use **linking words** to help you follow the argument. Some common linking words and expressions are *and, but, yet, however, also, later, alternatively, on the other hand, first, secondly, next, finally*. These linking words have different jobs to do. For example:

- *and, in addition, also* allow the writer to add more information

- *but, however, alternatively, on the other hand* suggest that the argument or line of thought is going to change direction

- *first, secondly, next, later, finally* can all suggest things happening in a specific order.

NOW TRY THIS

In the following newspaper article from the *Sunday Herald*, note how the linking words *but* and *however* help you to follow the argument, especially in the section called 'The debate'. Read the passage carefully and then answer all the questions, using your own words where asked to do so. Remember to use the skills you have learned so far in this chapter, as well as those you learned in Chapter 1.

Should the Voting Age be Lowered to 16?

Politicians from all sides worry that fewer people are turning out to vote, and about who's voting for who and why. So now is a good time to think about who
5   gets to vote and who doesn't. In fact, all over Europe, different groups are asking why 16-year-olds shouldn't be allowed to have their say in politics.

The debate

Here in Scotland, the Scottish Youth Parliament wants young people's voices to be
10   heard more in politics. 'It's a fundamental part of our manifesto to lower the voting age to 16,' says Youth Parliament Chair, Paul Kane. 'Turning 16 gives you enormous responsibilities – you can even get married. The government has a huge impact on your life, yet you can't vote for who represents you.' Political parties, such as The Scottish Greens, The Scottish Socialists, and the Scottish National Party, are among
15   those who have been campaigning (separately, of course) for years to reduce the voting age to 16 from the current 18. They all argue that since at age 16 a person is considered to be old enough to pay taxes, join the army to fight for their country or leave full-time education, then surely they are old enough to vote.

While the line has to be drawn somewhere, why is 18 currently the magic number?
20   Well, it's the age at which the UN define adulthood, and in most countries the voting age is 18. Other aspects of adulthood, such as being legally independent from your parents, and borrowing money, also happen at 18.

But in the 2001 General Election only 59.4% of possible voters turned out to have their say. Allowing 16-year-olds to vote might send a message to younger voters that
25   the government is worth taking an interest in. But does that mean it's the right move? The Scottish Conservatives are more interested in getting those who can already vote

to do so. According to a spokesperson: 'We don't believe that the case for a lowering of the age has been made and are content for it to remain at 18. It is more important for all politicians to give those who can vote a real reason for doing so.'

30 But Robin Harper MSP, a former teacher and leader of the Green Party in Scotland, believes the people who suggest that teenagers wouldn't use their vote just aren't communicating with young people.

'Of course 16-year-olds would use their vote,' he says. 'Right now, we're teaching children that democracy doesn't work, that their voices don't count. If they had more 35 input, they would learn that they can make a difference.' Harper also supports getting teenagers involved at a local council level. 'These teenagers are affected more than anyone by local council issues, such as youth projects, or sales of playing fields.'

However, many teenagers feel that they aren't ready to vote. Owen, studying Modern Studies Higher at Glasgow's St Aloysius' College, says: 'We do understand the 40 processes of politics, but not the policies of the parties.' His classmate Harriet agrees. 'It's just that we don't have the life experience,' she says.

A Nestlé Family Monitor/MORI poll in 2003 showed that 11 to 18-year-olds are interested in their local communities, but haven't much faith in the processes of national politics. So moving the voting age to 16 might force government to consider 45 policies affecting that age group more seriously.

However, there are other ways to get involved. Former youth parliament member, Holly, 17, from Ayr says 'The youth parliament is listened to in Holyrood. It's actually a better way to represent your age group than to have one vote.'

The result

There seems to be an attitude of 'if it ain't broke, don't fix it' among the British public 50 – around 60% of people support leaving the voting age at 18, in line with other rights of adulthood. But in parts of Germany and Austria, where a similar debate has been going on, 16 and 17-year-olds have been given the right to vote in local elections, although not in national ones. So hold on to your voting slips, perhaps the rest of the EU will follow suit.

Rosie Brown, *Sunday Herald*

Should the Voting Age be Lowered to 16? – Close Reading questions

Look again at lines 9–13.

1. **Explain in your own words** why Paul Kane thinks you should be able to vote at 16. 2 U

2. Quote the words which show how strongly Paul Kane feels about this, and explain how these words show the strength of his feelings. 2 A

3. Name two political parties that agree with him about this. 2 U

4. *'They all argue that since at age 16 a person is considered to be old enough to pay taxes, join the army to fight for their country or leave full-time education, then surely they are old enough to vote.'* (lines 16–18)

   How does the **sentence structure** here emphasise the strength of the argument? 2 A

5. Why is the question in line 19 a good way to start the paragraph? 2 A

6. **Using your own words as far as possible**, write down two things mentioned that young people can legally do at 18. 2 U

Look again at lines 23–29.

7. What point does the writer make in the first sentence of this paragraph? 2 U

8. How does the word '*But*' help to make clear the line of thought at this point? 2 A

9. According to the passage, which political party does *not* agree with the lowering of the voting age to 16? 1 U

10. **Using your own words as far as possible**, say what this party believes is the most important point. 2 U

11. Which word from lines 30–32 suggests that another point is going to be made in the argument? 1 A

12. Explain **in your own words** one point Robin Harper makes in lines 33–37. 2 U

13. What is surprising about the viewpoint of the teenagers in lines 38–41? Which word prepares you for this viewpoint? 2 U

Look at lines 49–54: **The result**

14. Explain **in your own words** what do most people in Britain feel about the issue. 2 U

15. What on the other hand, has happened in Germany and Austria? 2 U

16. Why is the last sentence a good way to finish the argument? 2 E

TOTAL – 30 marks

Link questions

Sometimes **linking words** are useful in answering **link questions**. **Link questions** often ask you to say how a sentence creates an effective **link** between one paragraph and another. Sometimes there is a **linking word or expression** there, and referring to it can form part of your answer. Some other expressions used to form links are words such as *this, that, these, those, it*. They are link words because they always refer back to something that has already been mentioned.

You usually need to answer link questions in two parts:

1. Show how one part **links back** to the previous paragraph.

2. Show how the other part **refers forward** to the new paragraph.

For example, there could have been a **link question** in the previous exercise like this:

> How does the sentence '*While the line has to be drawn somewhere, why is 18 the magic number?*' (line 19) effectively link this paragraph to what has gone before? **2 A**

A good answer to this would be:

The expression 'the line has to be drawn somewhere' links back to the ages at which you can and cannot do certain things, which was discussed in the previous paragraph.

The expression '... why is 18 the magic number?' asks the question which is going to be answered in the new paragraph.

This answer would get 2 marks because it has two parts to it, one linking back, the other referring forward.

We can put this into a **formula** for link questions which should ensure you always get 2 marks for this question.

Formula for link questions

The word/expression '_____' links back to _____ which was discussed in the previous paragraph.

The word/expression '_____' introduces the idea of _____ which is going to be discussed in the new paragraph.

NOW TRY THIS

The following article from the *Radio Times* was written to introduce a television programme about millionaires. Read the passage carefully and then answer all the questions, using your own words where asked to do so.

Mind of a Millionaire *causes atmosphere*

So you wanna be rich? Don't we all? But is it a question of luck who gets rich and who doesn't? That's the question posed by BBC 2's *Mind of a Millionaire*. As the
5   series demonstrates, luck has nothing to do with who becomes a millionaire. Interviews from tycoons as apparently disparate as Richard Bryson and Tom Hartley Junior (who made his first million
10 at 14 by selling luxury cars) show that self-made millionaires share important skills, values and abilities: a millionaire mindset. *↳ introducing list or something else*

So what is it that millionaires have in common? First, they're extremely single-minded. *— comparing* They're prepared to fight for success and to go round, over, under or through comet-
15 sized obstacles that would daunt the majority of us. Karl Watkin, a Geordie multi-millionaire, once applied for a job for which he only had one of the six qualifications that were needed. However, he was determined to get that job, and his drive and determination made sure that he did.

comparing again

It is no surprise that millionaires view success in financial terms. Research on 300
20 millionaires for the series found that 60 per cent rated the pursuit of financial success as more important than a happy love life. They enjoy spending money – however, *adds another* they're also extremely careful about their spending. They regard being ripped off as *point*

the ultimate humiliation. So they'll shop around on the gas bill, turn lights out when
they leave a room, look out for two-for-one offers and negotiate on purchases ranging
25 from cars to clothes. Designer gear doesn't feature too heavily on the millionaire
agenda, either: over half spend less than £500 per year on clothes – including
underwear and socks.

introduces another point

describing millionaires

This may be because they're too busy to shop. Millionaires are generally workaholics,
working an average 64-hour week, often longer. They don't have to work those hours
30 – many of them could spend the next 30 years doing nothing more strenuous than
the odd round of golf – but they choose to because they love their work. Karl Watkin
has a stunning country estate complete with a brand new swimming pool. However,
he's been in the pool only twice – one of those times was because he was pushed in.
He's too busy doing business on his mobile phone to have time for splashing around.

adds more description to part before

35 Another thing millionaires have in common is that most run their own businesses.
There could be several reasons for this. One is that they like to do things their own
way – and working in an organisation requires a conformity they can't abide. However,
they are also good at spotting the opportunities that others don't even notice. There's
nothing really original about a sushi bar, for instance, but Simon Woodroffe, founder
40 of Yo! Sushi, was the first to see the potential of a British chain.

There are many other common traits and values, but one that's crucial to success is
self-belief. That's what enables millionaires to take opportunities that others are too
timid to grasp. They stick with their dreams when others ridicule them. Ultimately, the
most vital ingredient in success is believing that you will succeed.

Sharon Maxwell Magnus, *Radio Times*

Mind of a Millionaire – Close Reading questions

1. How does the **sentence structure** of lines 1–3 make a good opening for the passage?   2 A

2. Write down another word from the first paragraph which means almost the same as 'millionaires'.   1 U

3. According to the writer in paragraph 1, what is *not* a factor in deciding who becomes a millionaire?   1 U

4. How does the sentence 'So what is it that millionaires have in common?' (line 13) create an effective **link** between paragraph two and paragraph three?   2 A

5. **Using your own words as far as possible,** say what is the first thing which millionaires have in common.   2 U

6. Show how the writer's **word choice** in 'comet-sized obstacles' makes us admire millionaires (lines 14–15).   2 A

7. How does the story of Karl Watkin's job application increase our admiration?   2 U

8. 'It is no surprise that millionaires view success in financial terms' (line 19). **In your own words** say what this sentence means.   2 U

9. What evidence does the writer use to back up this idea?   2 A

10. **Using your own words as far as possible,** write down two things millionaires will do to save money.   2 U

11. **In your own words,** say what is meant by the expression 'Designer gear doesn't feature too heavily on the millionaire agenda' (lines 25–26).   2 U

12. How does the **sentence structure** of lines 25–27 help you to understand what this expression means?   2 A

13. How does the sentence 'This may be because they're too busy to shop.' (line 28) provide an effective **link** between paragraphs 4 and 5?   2 A

14. Why does the writer use the expression 'splashing around' (line 34) instead of 'swimming'?   2 A

15. Look again at the paragraph starting at line 35. **Using your own words as far as possible,** write down two reasons why millionaires run their own businesses.   2 U

16. Explain how effective you find the final paragraph to be as a conclusion to the passage.   2 E

TOTAL – 30 marks

Evaluation questions

These last two exercises finished off with **Evaluation** questions. In Evaluation answers, you have to say how **good** or **effective** or **successful** or **appropriate** a particular piece of writing is. You may be asked, for instance:

- to comment on the **effectiveness** of a technique the writer uses

- to explain how **effective** you consider the ending of a passage to be.

There are usually about 4 or 5 marks for Evaluation, and they tend to be towards the end of the passage. They are often quite easy marks to gain as long as you remember that the SQA always choose well-written passages for you to answer questions on. Therefore you will usually be starting your answers with something like:

- *This is effective because…*

- *This is a good technique here because…*

You also have to **justify your answer**. In other words you have to give reasons for your answer.

NOW TRY THIS

In this extract from his travel book *Neither Here Nor There*, Bill Bryson writes in a humorous tone about his experiences of traffic in Paris. Read the passage carefully and then answer all the questions, using your own words where asked to do so.

Crossing the Road in Paris

In the morning I got up early and went for a long walk through the sleeping streets. I love to watch cities wake up, and Paris wakes up more abruptly, more startlingly, than any place I know. One minute you have the city to yourself: it's just you and a guy delivering crates of bread, and a couple of droning street-cleaning machines. (It might
5 be worth noting here that Paris spends £58 a year a head on street-cleaning compared with £17 a head in London, which explains why Paris gleams and London is a toilet.) Then all at once it's frantic: cars and buses swishing past, cafés and kiosks opening, people flying out of Metro stations like flocks of startled birds, movement everywhere, thousands and thousands of pairs of hurrying legs.

10 By half-past eight Paris is a terrible place for walking. There's too much traffic. A blue haze of diesel hangs over every boulevard. I know Baron Haussmann made Paris a grand place to look at, but the man had no concept of traffic flow. At the Arc de Triomphe alone thirteen roads come together. Is that asking for trouble or what?

It's interesting to note that the French have had a reputation for bad driving since long
15 before the invention of the internal combustion engine. Even in the eighteenth century British travellers to Paris were remarking on what lunatic drivers the French were, on 'the astonishing speed with which the carriages and people moved through the streets … It was not an uncommon sight to see a child run over and probably killed.'

You also constantly keep coming up against these monumental squares and open
20 spaces that are nearly impossible to cross on foot. My wife and I went to Paris on our
honeymoon and foolishly tried to cross the Place de la Concorde. Somehow she
managed to get to the obelisk in the centre, but I was stranded in the midst of a
circus of killer automobiles, waving weakly to my dear spouse of two days and
whimpering softly while hundreds and hundreds of little buff-coloured Renaults were
25 bearing down on me with their drivers all wearing expressions like Jack Nicholson in
Batman.

It still happens now. At the Place de la Bastille, a vast open space, I spent three-
quarters of an hour trying to get from the Rue de Lyon to the Rue de St-Antoine. The
problem is that the pedestrian-crossing lights have been designed with the clear
30 purpose of leaving the foreign visitor confused, humiliated and, if all goes to plan,
dead.

This is what happens: you arrive at a square to find all the traffic stopped, but the
pedestrian light is red and you know that if you venture so much as a foot off the
kerb all the cars will surge forward and turn you into a gooey pancake. So you wait.
35 After a minute, a blind person comes along and crosses the great cobbled plain
without hesitating. Then a ninety-year-old lady in a motorized wheelchair trundles
past and wobbles across the cobbles to the other side of the square a quarter of a
mile away.

You are uncomfortably aware that all the drivers within 150 yards are sitting with
40 moistened lips watching you expectantly, so you pretend that you don't really want to
cross the street at all, that actually you've come over here to look at this interesting
lamppost. Finally, the pedestrian light turns green and you step off the kerb and all
the cars come charging at you. And I don't care how paranoid and irrational this
sounds, but I know for a fact that the people of Paris want me dead.

Bill Bryson, *Neither Here Nor There – Travels in Europe*

Crossing the Road in Paris – Close Reading questions

1. Look again at lines 1–3. **In your own words,** say what the writer likes doing and how Paris is different from other cities. **2 U**

2. What evidence does the writer give in lines 3–4 to expand on the idea that *'One minute you have the city to yourself'*? **1 A**

3. Quote **one** piece of evidence the writer gives to show that *'Then all at once it's frantic'*. **1 A**

4. What is the function of the **colons** in lines 3 and 7? **1 A**

5. Why is the **choice** of the **word** '*droning*' in line 4 effective in describing the street-cleaning machines? 2 A

6. '*London is a toilet.*' (line 6)

   What does this image suggest about the state of London's streets? 2 A

7. Look again at lines 10–13. **In your own words**, give two reasons why '*Paris is a terrible place for walking*' by half-past eight. 2 U

8. Bill Bryson uses a **question** at the end of the second paragraph (lines 10–13). Why do you think he asks a question at this point? 2 A

9. Look again at lines 14–18. What is the main reason Bill Bryson gives for French drivers' bad reputation? 1 U

10. Look again at lines 19–20. **In your own words**, say why crossing the road is difficult. 2 U

11. '*... waving weakly to my dear spouse of two days and whimpering softly while hundreds and hundreds of little buff-coloured Renaults were bearing down on me with their drivers all wearing expressions like Jack Nicholson in Batman.*' (lines 23–26)

    Several **language techniques** used in these lines show the difficulty of his situation in a funny way. Choose **two** of the following **language techniques**.

    In each case quote the word or expression you are going to deal with and then make a comment to show how it makes clear his difficulties in a humorous way.

    Word choice

    Imagery

    Exaggeration

    Sound 4 A

12. '*The problem is that the pedestrian-crossing lights have been designed with the clear purpose of leaving the foreign visitor confused, humiliated and, if all goes to plan, dead.*' (lines 28–31)

    Quote the word in these lines which tells you that Bill Bryson is not writing an absolutely serious article and explain why the word you have chosen cannot be serious. 2 A

13. Look again at lines 32–34. '*This is what happens*'. According to Bill Bryson what **three** things happen? 3 U

14. What **two** things happen in lines 35–38 which seem to prove him wrong? 2 U

15. What finally happens to him when he steps off the pavement? 1 U

16. Give **two** reasons for the last sentence (lines 43–44) being a neat and effective ending to this passage. 2 E

TOTAL – 30 marks

Punctuation marks

In question 2 above, you were asked about the function of the **colon** – the job that the colon does in the sentence. If you have completed Chapter 1, you will remember that we did some work on punctuation in the **sentence structure** section (pages 17–18). There we learned about the **dash** being used to introduce a list or an example. The **colon** can also be used to introduce a list or example or explanation.

Below is a list of some of the different punctuation marks and their uses.

Comma	,	■ to separate items in a list
Pair of commas	, ... ,	■ to mark off an extra piece of information – the information goes between the commas
Dash	–	■ to introduce a list, example or explanation
Pair of dashes	– ...... –	■ to mark off an extra piece of information
Brackets	(......)	■ to mark off an extra piece of information – the information goes between the brackets
Colon	:	■ to introduce a list, example or explanation
CAPITALS		■ to emphasise something important ■ to suggest the way something is said
Italics		■ to emphasise something important ■ to suggest the way something is said ■ to indicate the name of a book, film, etc.
Inverted commas **speech marks** **quotation marks**	'......' "......"	■ to indicate exact words spoken ■ to suggest "so called" use of expression For example the sentence: *He was a 'hero'* suggests that he wasn't really a hero at all. The word is being used in a particular way here, ironically or sarcastically.

NOW TRY THIS

In this extract from his autobiography the champion cyclist Lance Armstrong, winner of the famous Tour de France for a record seven times, writes about his cycling and his fight against cancer. Read the passage carefully and then answer all the questions, using your own words where asked to do so.

It's Not About the Bike

I want to die at a hundred years old with an American flag on my back and the star of Texas on my helmet, after screaming down an Alpine descent on a bicycle at
5   75 miles per hour. I want to cross one last finish line as my wife and my ten children applaud, and then I want to lie down in a field of those famous French sunflowers and gracefully expire.

10 A slow death is not for me. I don't do anything slow, not even breathe. I do everything at a fast pace: eat fast, sleep fast. It makes me crazy when my wife, Kristin, drives our car, because she brakes at all the yellow caution lights, while I squirm impatiently in the passenger seat.

I've spent my life racing my bike, from the back roads of Austin, Texas to the Champs-
15 Elysées in Paris, and I always figured if I died an untimely death, it would be because some rancher in his Dodge 4×4 ran me headfirst into a ditch. Believe me, it could happen. Cyclists fight an ongoing war with guys in big trucks, and so many vehicles have hit me, so many times, in so many countries, I've lost count. I've learned how to take out my own stitches: all you need is a pair of fingernail clippers and a strong
20 stomach.

If you saw my body underneath my racing jersey, you'd know what I'm talking about. I've got marbled scars on both arms and discolored marks up and down my legs, which I keep clean-shaven. Maybe that's why trucks are always trying to run me over; they see my sissy-boy calves and decide not to brake. But cyclists have to shave,
25 because when the gravel gets into your skin, it's easier to clean and bandage if you have no hair.

One minute you're pedaling along a highway, and the next minute, *boom*, you're face-down in the dirt. A blast of hot air hits you, you taste the acrid, oily exhaust in the roof of your mouth, and all you can do is wave a fist at the disappearing taillights.

30 Cancer was like that. It was like being run off the road by a truck, and I've got the scars to prove it. There's a puckered wound in my upper chest just above my heart, which is where the catheter was implanted. A surgical line runs from the right side of my groin into my upper thigh, where they cut out my testicle. But the real prizes are two deep half-moons in my scalp, as if I was kicked twice in the head by a horse.

35 Those are the leftovers from brain surgery.

When I was 25, I got testicular cancer and nearly died. I was given less than a 40 percent chance of surviving, and frankly, some of my doctors were just being kind when they gave me those odds.

Some of the events are not easy to tell or comfortable to hear. I'm asking you now, at
40 the outset, to put aside your ideas about heroes and miracles, because I'm not storybook material, even if I did win the Tour de France. This is not Disneyland, or Hollywood. I'll give you an example: I've read that I *flew* up the hills and mountains of France. But you don't fly up a hill. You struggle slowly and painfully up a hill, and maybe, if you work very hard, you get to the top ahead of everybody else.

45 Cancer is like that, too. Good, strong people get cancer, and they do all the right things to beat it, and they still die. That is the essential truth that you learn. People die. And after you learn it, all other matters seem irrelevant. They just seem small.

I don't know why I'm still alive. I can only guess. I have a tough constitution, and my profession taught me how to compete against long odds and big obstacles. I like to
50 train hard and I like to race hard. That helped, it was a good start, but it certainly wasn't the determining factor. I can't help feeling that my survival was more a matter of blind luck.

Lance Armstrong, *It's Not About the Bike: My Journey Back to Life*

It's Not About the Bike – Close Reading questions

1. Look again at the first two paragraphs, lines 1–13. Which **four** of the following **contrasting** words indicate how Lance Armstrong says he wants to die? *fast/slow young/old cycling/driving single/married* **2 U**

2. What is meant by the word *'expire'* in line 9? How does the **context** help you to arrive at that meaning? **2 U**

3. *'It makes me crazy when my wife, Kristin, drives our car, because she brakes at all the yellow caution light, while I squirm impatiently in the passenger seat.'* (lines 11–13)

   From what you have read in lines 10–11, why do you think Lance Armstrong *'squirm(s) impatiently in the passenger seat'*? **2   U**

4. Look again at lines 14–18. Explain **in your own words** the way in which Lance Armstrong thought he might die early. **2   U**

5. What is the purpose of the **colon** in line 19? **2   A**

6. How does the writer's **word choice** in line 16 help you to realise what it must be like to take out your own stitches? **2   A**

7. *'If you saw my body underneath my racing jersey, you'd know what I'm talking about.'* (lines 19–20)

   Show how this sentence is an effective beginning to the paragraph. **2   A**

8. Look again at lines 22–26. Explain in your own words why Lance Armstrong shaves his legs. **2   U**

9. *'Cancer was like that.'* (line 30) Why do you think this sentence is short? **2   A**

10. *'It was like being run off the road by a truck…'* (line 30)

    How does this **comparison** highlight the effect of the cancer? **2   A**

11. Quote another **comparison** from later in this paragraph, and explain how it shows the dramatic effect of his cancer. **2   A**

12. **In your own words** say what the writer means by *'some of my doctors were just being kind when they gave me these odds'* (lines 37–38). **1   U**

13. Why do you think the writer refers to *'Disneyland or Hollywood'* when he is talking about his life story? **2   A**

14. The writer makes use of **contrast** in lines 42–44. Quote two words or expressions that show the contrast and say how effective you think the contrast is. **2   E**

15. Read lines 45–47 again. Quote one sentence from this paragraph which you think is effective in convincing the reader about the reality of cancer, and why you think it is effective. **2   A**

16. This extract comes from an autobiography called *It's Not About the Bike*. What do you think the book *is* about? **1   U**

   TOTAL – 30 marks

NOW TRY THIS

In this extract from his autobiography *Toast: The Story of a Boy's Hunger*, cookery writer Nigel Slater writes about the annual making of the family Christmas cake when he was a boy. Read the passage carefully and then answer all the questions, using your own words where asked to do so.

Christmas Cake

Mum never was much of a cook. Meals arrived on the table as much by happy accident as by domestic science. She was a chops-and-peas sort of a cook,
5 occasionally going so far as to make a rice pudding. She found it all a bit of an ordeal.

Once a year there were Christmas puddings and cakes to be made. They
10 were made with neither love nor joy.
They simply had to be done. 'I suppose I had better DO THE CAKE,' she would sigh. The food mixer – she was not the sort of woman to use her hands – was an ancient, heavy Kenwood that lived in a deep, secret hole in the kitchen work surface. My father had, in a rare moment of do-it-yourselfery, fitted a heavy industrial spring
15 under the mixer so that when you lifted the lid the mixer slowly rose like a corpse from a coffin.

She never quite got the hang of the mixer. I can picture her now, desperately trying to harness her wayward Kenwood, bits of cake mixture flying out of the bowl like something from an *I Love Lucy* sketch.

20 Cooks know to butter and line the cake tins before they start the creaming and beating. My mother would remember just before she put the final spoonful of brandy into the cake mixture, then take half an hour to find them. They always turned up in a drawer, rusty and full of fluff. Then there was the annual scrabble to find the brown paper, the scissors, the string. However much she hated making the cake we both
25 loved the sound of the raw cake mixture falling into the tin. 'Shhh, listen to the cake mixture,' she would say, and the two of us would listen to the slow plop of the dollops of fruit and butter and sugar falling into the paper-lined cake tin. The kitchen would be warmer than usual and my mother would have that I've-just-baked-a-cake glow. 'Oh, put a record on, will you, dear? Put some carols on,' she would say as she
30 put the cake in the oven. Carols or not, it always sank in the middle, the

embarrassing hollow, sometimes as deep as your fist, having to be filled in with marzipan.

Forget scented candles and freshly brewed coffee. Every home should smell of baking Christmas cake. It was a pity we had Auntie Jenny living with us. Her incontinence
35 could take the edge off the smell of a chicken curry, let alone a baking cake. No matter how many mince pies were being made, or pine logs burning in the grate, or how many orange-and-clove pomanders my mother had made, there was always the faintest whiff of Auntie Jenny.

Warm sweet fruit, a cake in the oven, woodsmoke, warm ironing, hot retriever, mince
40 pies. Every child's Christmas memories should smell like that. Mine did. It is a pity that there was always a passing breeze of ammonia.

Cake holds a family together. I really believed it did. My father was a different man when there was cake in the house. Warm. The sort of man I wanted to hug rather than shy away from. If he had a plate of cake in his hand I knew it would be all right to
45 climb up on to his lap. There was something about the way my mother put a cake on the table that made me feel that all was well. Safe. Secure. Unshakeable. Even when she got to the point where she carried her Ventolin inhaler in her left hand all the time. Unshakeable. Even when she and my father used to go for long walks, walking ahead of me and talking in hushed tones and he would come back with tears in his eyes.

50 When I was eight my mother's annual attempt at icing the family Christmas cake was handed over to me. 'I've had enough of this lark, dear, you're old enough now.' She had started to sit down a lot. I made only marginally less of a mess than she did, but at least I didn't cover the table, the floor, the dog with icing sugar. To be honest, it was a relief to get it out of her hands. I followed the Slater house style of snowy peaks
55 brought up with the flat of a knife and a red ribbon. Even then I wasn't one to rock the boat. The idea behind the wave effect of her icing was simply to hide the fact that her attempt at covering the cake in marzipan resembled nothing more than an unmade bed. Folds and lumps, creases and tears. A few patches stuck on with a bit of apricot jam.

I knew I could have probably have flat-iced a cake to perfection, but to have done so
60 would have hurt her feelings. So waves it was. There was also a chipped Father Christmas, complete with a jagged lump of last year's marzipan round his feet, and the dusty bristle tree with its snowy tips of icing. I drew the line at the fluffy yellow Easter chick.

Baking a cake for your family to share, the stirring of cherries, currants, raisins, peel
65 and brandy, brown sugar, butter, eggs and flour, for me the ultimate symbol of a mother's love for her husband and kids, was reduced to something that 'simply has to be done'. Like cleaning the loo or polishing the shoes.

Nigel Slater, *Toast*

Christmas Cake – Close Reading questions

1. Quote two pieces of evidence from the first paragraph which show that the author's mother did not like cooking. **2 U**

2. What is the effect of the capitals in 'I suppose I had better DO THE CAKE' (line 11)? **2 A**

3. What is the effect of the expression within the pair of dashes in line 12: '– she was not the sort of woman to use her hands –'? **2 A**

4. Quote an example of **personification** or **simile** about the mixer from lines 12–16 and say what impression it gives of the mixer. **2 A**

5. Look again at lines 20–24. **In your own words,** write down two pieces of evidence that show his mother was disorganised. **2 U**

6. '… the two of us would listen to the slow plop of the dollops of fruit and butter and sugar falling into the paper-lined cake tin.' (lines 23–24)

   Choose one **language technique** used here. Name the technique and say why it helps to describe the incident well. **2 A**

7. '… my mother would have that I've-just-baked-a-cake glow.' (lines 28–29). What is the effect of the underlined expression here? **2 A**

8. Read lines 33–38. Quote two of the smells which the writer liked in his house at Christmas time. **2 U**

9. In lines 39–41 the writer again mentions some of the pleasant smells he remembers. Show how **sentence structure** helps to emphasise these. **2 A**

10. Look again at lines 42–46. **Using your own words**, say how the presence of cake in the house affected his relationship with

    a) his father
    b) his mother. **2 U**

11. Read lines 46–49. Write down **in your own words** two signs that show that there were problems in the Slater household. **2 U**

12. In lines 50–52 you are given a clue about why his mother handed over the icing of the cake to her son. Quote the clue and write down what it lets you know. **2 A**

13. The marzipan covering of the cake is said to look like 'an unmade bed' (line 57). Quote two words which the writer has chosen to add to this picture. Why are they good words to use here? **2 A**

14. Why does the writer say 'I drew the line at the fluffy yellow Easter chick' (lines 62–63)? **1 U**

15. The writer uses **contrast** in the last paragraph (lines 64–67). Explain what the contrast is and say how effective you find the final paragraph in bringing the extract to a conclusion. **3 E**

TOTAL – 30 marks

You've now practised most of the language techniques and types of questions needed to pass the Close Reading NAB and Close Reading paper in the SQA exam. Each NAB or exam paper will be different, but all will have the same types of questions. All you need in addition is careful, detailed reading and a fair amount of your own common sense. Don't forget to keep on reading the kind of texts mentioned at the beginning of this chapter, building on your vocabulary, and making sure you can follow the line of thought.

3 Prose: Snakes And Ladders

The three types of literature you can write essays about in the exam are called **drama**, **poetry** and **prose**. You probably know that writing about **drama** means showing your knowledge about the script of a play. You certainly know what **poetry** is, and you will find three poems and work to go with them in Chapters 6–8 of this book. Do you know the word **prose** though?

Prose just describes any piece of writing that is written in sentences and paragraphs. It could be a news story, a diary, a letter or a cookery book. In the Intermediate 1 course the two sorts of **fictional** (imaginative or made up) prose that you might study are **novels** (stories in chapters where one story fills up a whole book) and **short stories**.

 GETTING IN

We're going to look at a short story in a moment. It's mostly set in a council office. Before you read the story, think about the following questions. You should share your answers with a partner, a small group, or your class.

- Have you ever had to meet with an official or important person at their workplace?

- How did you feel during this meeting?

- Did the meeting go the way you wanted it to?

 FIRST THOUGHTS

As you read it through for the first time, think about the answers to these two questions:

- Who is the main character in this story?
- How much time does the story cover?

Snakes and Ladders

1. Lily picked at the hem of her coat sleeve while she waited. She was wearing her good coat today – at least, it used to be good but now it was fraying at the cuffs. Since Sammy went into hospital she had been losing weight and her clothes, as well as being shabby, drooped over her narrow shoulders. It didn't seem worth cooking a proper dinner just for one, and besides, skipping meals saved money. Not that there was ever any to save.

2. The waiting room smelled of disinfectant, like the hospital. The doctors there told her, when she could get hold of one, that Sammy was making some improvement but she didn't notice any. The therapist said that he was interested in clay and had him throwing fistfuls of it at the wall. Something about frustration, the therapist said, but there was more to it than that. Everyone in her area must be frustrated if frustration meant throwing things. There were broken windows all over. Sammy would be normal if that was all there was to it. They were giving him drugs to regulate his behaviour – that's what they said – but the drugs just made him talk a lot of nonsense or loll around with his mouth hanging open. He was like a lump of clay himself on those sedatives. He still screamed if anyone mentioned a cupboard. One day he threw himself at the wall.

3. 'Number eight, please.' A thin woman got up, tugging at the man next to her. He grunted, heaved to his feet and slouched after her through the door marked INTERVIEWS. The door clicked shut. Lily's plastic card had a nine on it so she would be next. She bit a ragnail and fixed her eyes on a poster directly opposite her. There was nothing else to look at. In large black letters it commanded:

TAKE PRIDE IN YOUR ENVIRONMENT
DON'T SPOIL IT WITH LITTER

4. The words were printed on a stretch of very green grass, sprinkled with daisies. Right in the middle of the meadow lay a pile of crisp packets and broken beer bottles. Who'd want to spoil such lovely grass? Lily couldn't remember seeing grass which looked as green. There was nothing in the poster which looked at all like Lily's area except the litter, though even that looked wrong. You could sweep that up in a minute. Litter, as Lily knew it, meant streets of rotting filth which spewed out of

drains every time it rained and crawled further and further up the walls of the flats. And the grass wasn't green like that. It was nearer the colour of dishwater.

5. 'Number nine, please.' The number eight people slammed the waiting-room door behind them as they left. Lily went into the interview room, holding out her number. The young clerk coughed briskly into his fist. He scraped his chair forward until he was tucked in tightly behind his desk. He began thumbing through a pile of forms. Lily smiled, noting that his shirt was missing a button. Needs looking after, she thought, just like Sammy.

6. 'Now then, your name is Marsh, Lily Marsh, is that correct?' The clerk spread his arms across the polished wood and leaned towards Lily. She nodded in reply.

7. 'And you're divorced, Mrs Marsh, am I right? And reside at 125 Hill View, 14B, Easter Drumbeath?'

8. 'Yes.'

9. 'And I understand you've applied for a transfer?'

10. 'That's right. I want to move to another area.'

11. The clerk pulled a green form from the pile. It was a dull colour, a bit like the doors on the flats at her end of Hill View, where you couldn't see the hills. You could see the quarry though, a great lake of yellow mud. The council had re-painted the doors on the other end of the street a year past, but they'd stopped halfway.

12. 'You see, my son's no well. He's in the hospital. He had a terrible shock ...' At that moment the clerk was overwhelmed by a fit of sneezing. 'You should be in your bed,' said Lily. The young man coughed, then gave her a bleary smile.

13. 'Yes I ... no I'm afraid ... some of us must keep going,' he replied, as though remembering a motto. He straightened up his papers.

14. 'Now, can we go through this step by step, if you please.' He glanced at the clock while he spoke. 'You say your son resides with you?'

15. 'He stays with me, yes. But we cannae go on staying where we are.'

16. The clerk sighed, stubbed his pencil against the desk, took a deep breath. 'I'm aware Easter Drumbeath is not the most desirable housing area but there's a long list for houses anywhere. Easter Drumbeath houses forty thousand tenants and I would say, at a modest estimate, twenty per cent of them have applied for a transfer within the last five years. Do you know how many people that is Mrs Marsh? Thousands!'

17. 'I know it's hard for other people in Drum. The place is in a terrible state. It's like ...' her fingers twisted into her cuffs, 'like the inside of a litter bin.'

18. 'Ah but you see, the council cannot be held responsible for litter. After all, who drops the litter?'

19. 'It's not just that,' Lily began, but the clerk still had his eye on the clock.

20. 'I must explain to you that the council allocates rehousing through what we call a point system.' He raised his eyes to the ceiling, as though he were trying to remember his lines. 'This is based on the present condition of the tenant's housing. I must emphasise that the waiting list is extremely long and, in all fairness, would be better closed for the time being. Even if your points do add up to the required number, it is likely to be a considerable time before the relocation takes place. With the situation as it is, it would be better not to raise people's hopes. Do you see what I mean, Mrs Marsh?'

21. The clerk peered at Lily with such weary eyes that she felt obliged to nod, although she wanted to ask about the points system and relocation and how long a 'considerable time' was likely to be. But she didn't want to be a nuisance.

22. 'Let's start with you Mrs Marsh. Do you work?'

23. 'No.'

24. 'What about your ex-husband? Does he provide any maintenance?' Lily answered the first string of questions to the top of the clerk's head while he ticked off boxes on the green form.

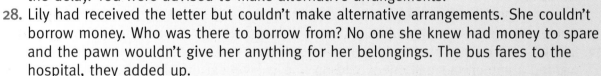

25. 'I have a note here to the effect that you are behind with your rent payments.'

26. 'It's only three weeks behind,' she replied. 'It's the first time. You see my son's in the hospital and the new payment scheme's not working properly yet.'

27. 'There was a circular, Mrs Marsh, supplying advance information relating to the delay. You were advised to make alternative arrangements.'

28. Lily had received the letter but couldn't make alternative arrangements. She couldn't borrow money. Who was there to borrow from? No one she knew had money to spare and the pawn wouldn't give her anything for her belongings. The bus fares to the hospital, they added up.

29. 'Still,' said the clerk, 'I imagine many people in Easter Drumbeath are in the same position. We'll try to find out what can be said in your favour, shall we? For instance, if you are lacking in some basic amenity, like a clean water supply or electricity, it would be easier to push a transfer through.'

30. 'They're going to cut off my electricity soon. I can't pay the bill.' Lily hadn't intended to mention the electric but the clerk seemed to be saying that having it cut off would help.

31. 'I'm afraid that's no good, Mrs Marsh. If it had already been cut off, it might have made a difference, but we can only take the present situation into consideration.'

32. 'But the flats are damp,' said Lily. 'I've got to keep the fire on all the time. There's damp all over the walls, in big black patches.' The clerk took note of this. The word 'damp' was given a tick. One point to Lily. It was as if the two of them were playing a strange game of snakes and ladders, with Lily landing on more than her fair share of snakes. When the clerk reached the bottom of the third page of questions, there remained a small space without any boxes.

33. 'He had a breakdown, my son Sammy. He had a terrible shock and then he had a breakdown.' She paused. Would there be room for any more?

34. 'Go on Mrs Marsh.'

35. 'There was this empty flat ... on the floor below. Sammy used to go there sometimes to ... just to look round, for something to do ...' She couldn't say that he brought her floorboards for firewood. 'He was poking around, just looking at things. He'd told me about a funny smell coming from a cupboard. I said it would be the damp because

everything smells rotten when it's damp. The cupboard was locked. I said he shouldn't force it, I told him to leave well alone. But you know what kids are like. He got the door open. And there he was!'

36. 'Who was, Mrs Marsh?'

37. 'Mr Martin, from flat eleven, hanging from a rope, poor man. There were ... things moving all over him. Poor Sammy. Poor Mr Martin. Sorry!' Lily choked to a halt.

38. The young man was embarrassed by the weeping woman in front of him but he had come across this kind of thing before. Sometimes it was just a try-on.

39. 'So this ah ... this breakdown you say your son had, this would have occurred as a result ... of the shock of seeing this, ah ... corpse?' Lily lowered her head. 'I do sympathise with you Mrs Marsh. I'll try to do what I ...' The clerk's condolences were cut short by another irrepressible sneeze.

40. Lily walked home along the canal. It was a long walk but it helped to pass the time. It was a bright day and the sun stroked the back of her neck like a warm fingertip. Towards the end of the landscaped walkway, she began to start noticing the litter. A piece of broken bottle had trapped the sun on its curve and shone fiercely. A wisp of smoke curled round the jagged edge. Below the glass, the weeds were scorched.

41. She climbed through the torn fence where Easter Drumbeath's tangle of cement walkways snaked across the motorway. This was where the gardens abruptly came to an end, where the birdsong petered out. In Drumbeath the birds didn't stay long, except for the scavenging gulls: and they didn't sing, they squawked.

42. She glanced back at the neat bungalows and their well-tended lawns. She'd always wanted a garden, a small one would do fine, a lawn set off with a blaze of colour in

the flowerbeds. But they'd never give her a garden. On the path, the broken bottle had started a small fire. How easy that would be, she thought. She'd heard of folk who'd done such things.

43. When she arrived at the centre, she counted out her change and stopped at one of the few shops which wasn't an off-licence or a betting shop. A row of fortresses, grilled and barred with iron. No one wanted a shop here any more. The insurance was too high, the break-ins too frequent, even with the iron bars and electronic alarms. She pushed open the heavy door.

44. The man behind the counter was filling in a pools coupon and smoking between coughs. On the counter lay a pile of shrivelled oranges next to slabs of sausage meat and discoloured bacon. The radio crackled out a song about the bright city lights of somewhere else.

45. 'Yeah,' said the shopkeeper without looking up.

46. 'How much is a gallon of paraffin?' Lily asked, as casually as possible.

Dilys Rose

THINKING THROUGH

First, share your answers to the **First Thoughts** questions you were given at the start of the story. Then work out the answers to the following three questions:

1. Who is Sammy?

2. What caused his mental breakdown?

3. What is Lily planning to do, and why?

LET'S GET TO WORK

You might think that not a lot happens in the story. But actually, it is an effective story because it makes us feel sympathy. As we study this story we are going to look mainly at the characters, and at the settings. Most of the sympathy we end up feeling for Lily, the main character, comes about because we realise how miserable she is because of the setting she has to live in. Sammy's breakdown too is caused by something that happened to him because of the setting he and his mother live in.

Characters

We are going to start by examining the housing clerk. In many ways he might seem to be the 'bad guy' in the story, and we'll begin with some of his more unpleasant features.

In paragraph 20 we are told the clerk:

> 'raised his eyes to the ceiling, as though he were trying to remember his lines.'

This tells us a lot about the way that he approaches his job and his clients. He probably finds his work boring and repetitive. Unfortunately this means that he's not interested in people like Lily when they come to see him. He doesn't seem to be able to treat his clients as individuals. Instead he works through pre-prepared speeches and pre-set questions, treating everyone the same.

NOW TRY THIS

Look at paragraphs 5, 13 and 14.

1. Which words and phrases tell us that the clerk is rather tense?

If the clerk just seemed tense and nervous, we might just think he was a shy young man. However, one of the most unpleasant things about the clerk is the suspicious way he thinks about the people who come to ask for his help.

2. Look at paragraph 18. How does the clerk try to blame the Drumbeath residents for their environment?
3. Look at paragraph 38. What does the clerk suspect about Lily?

We often get the impression that he can't wait for the interview to be over. In paragraph 14 we are told:

> 'He glanced at the clock while he spoke.'

Also throughout the interview, the clerk often behaves in quite a rude manner, or seems to be trying to ignore Lily even while she is sitting in front of him.

NOW TRY THIS

Look again at paragraphs 16, 19–20 and 24. In each one, pick out the detail showing his rude actions. In some cases you could quote, but in others it may be easier to explain briefly in your own words what he does.

All the way through their interview, the clerk uses very **formal language**. We sometimes use the word **register** to describe this choice, so we could also say that the clerk speaks in the **formal register**, while Lily's register is more **informal**. Using this kind of very impersonal language is one way that the clerk keeps Lily at a distance.

NOW TRY THIS

A lot of what the clerk says can be re-written in 'normal' English – not slang but something a little more everyday. For example:

> *'Now then, your name is Marsh, Lily Marsh, is that correct?'*

could be re-written to say:

> *'Your name is Lily Marsh isn't it?'*

Now try to re-write these things the clerk says to Lily:

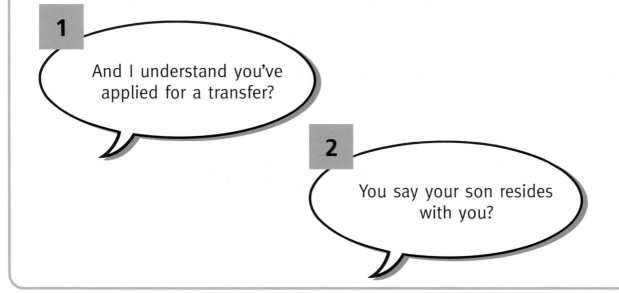

1 And I understand you've applied for a transfer?

2 You say your son resides with you?

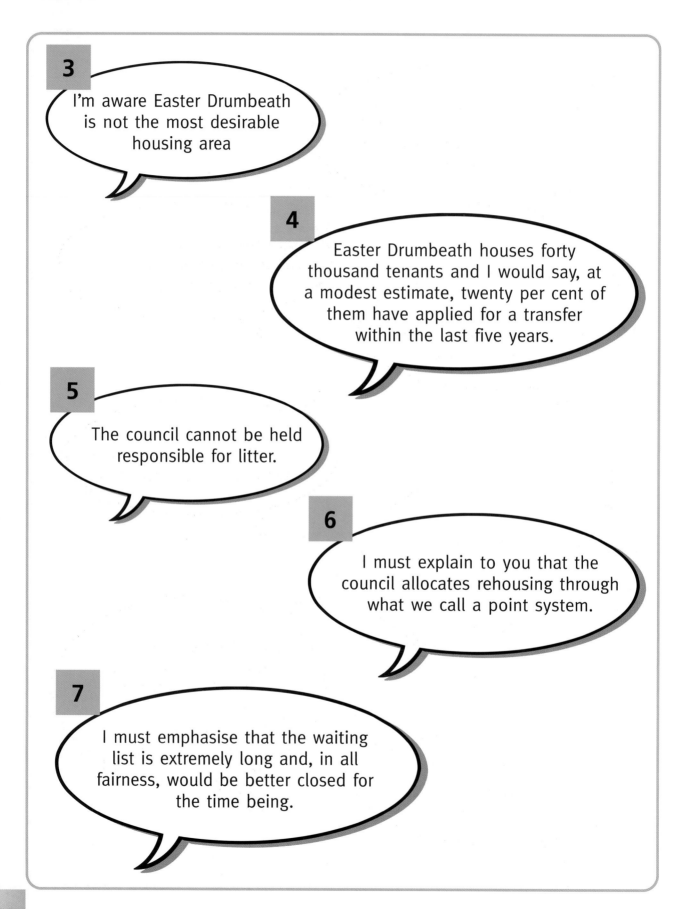

3 I'm aware Easter Drumbeath is not the most desirable housing area

4 Easter Drumbeath houses forty thousand tenants and I would say, at a modest estimate, twenty per cent of them have applied for a transfer within the last five years.

5 The council cannot be held responsible for litter.

6 I must explain to you that the council allocates rehousing through what we call a point system.

7 I must emphasise that the waiting list is extremely long and, in all fairness, would be better closed for the time being.

8 Even if your points do add up to the required number, it is likely to be a considerable time before the relocation takes place.

9 With the situation as it is, it would be better not to raise people's hopes.

10 What about your ex-husband? Does he provide any maintenance?

11 I have a note here to the effect that you are behind with your rent payments.

12 There was a circular, Mrs Marsh, supplying advance information relating to the delay. You were advised to make alternative arrangements.

13 For instance, if you are lacking in some basic amenity, like a clean water supply or electricity, it would be easier to push a transfer through.

14 We can only take the present situation into consideration.

We do not know what the clerk says to Lily at the end of their meeting. He must say something to get her to leave, but the last thing we are told about him is that he starts to sneeze.

NOW TRY THIS

Using your knowledge of the way he speaks, and using formal language, write what you think the clerk said to Lily to let her know the interview is over.

As well as bombarding her with important-sounding formal language, the clerk also attempts to blind Lily with numbers.

NOW TRY THIS

Answer the following questions:

1. Look again at what the clerk says in paragraph 16. You might need to use a calculator for this bit. How many people in Easter Drumbeath have actually applied for a transfer in the last five years?
2. Why do you think the clerk doesn't tell Lily the actual number?
3. Is he trying to impress her with huge numbers?
4. Does he think she's not clever enough to work out the answer?
5. Or is he, perhaps, not clever enough to work it out?

So far we've looked at the bad side of the clerk. However, Dilys Rose, the writer, doesn't want to create someone who is totally bad. Although he doesn't have the same problems as the council tenants who come to his office, there are details in the story to make the reader feel that the clerk may be in need of some sympathy too.

The whole story is told from Lily's point of view. We follow her thoughts and tend to 'agree' with her. In order to make us believe that the clerk deserves a little of our compassion, the writer gets Lily to notice some details about him.

1. What does Lily notice about him in paragraph 5?
2. Who does she compare the clerk with in her mind?
3. Why is it important that she compares him to this person in particular?

Rose also gives the clerk a severe cold. This makes us think that perhaps he would do his job better, or be kinder to his clients, if he wasn't feeling so ill. Perhaps we even respect him a little for coming in to work and being there to see Lily on a day when he'd probably rather be at home in bed.

Skim through the story. Make a note of every time the clerk's illness is mentioned, or everything he does that could be a symptom of his cold.

Before we leave the clerk behind, it's worth noticing that he has all the power in this situation, and that this power makes Lily even more nervous. Most obviously, either he actually has the power to give Lily a new and better flat, or at least she believes that he has the power to do so, which amounts to the same thing.

Also, when Lily goes in for her meeting with him, the clerk already knows a lot about her. There is a well-known expression that tells us, 'Knowledge is power.' The clerk doesn't just know her name and address and the fact that she wants a transfer. He also knows much more personal information like the fact that Lily is divorced. Later on we find him using a piece of information that could be very embarrassing or humiliating for Lily: the fact that she is behind with her rent.

NOW TRY THIS

Now that you have thought in detail about the character of the clerk, brainstorm as many words as you can think of to describe him.

Having had a good look at the clerk, it's time to examine Lily, the main character of the story. We're going to especially look at Dilys Rose's **characterisation** of Lily. *Characterisation* just means all the things an author does to build up a character and make that person seem real. We come to see the character in a certain way because of all the techniques and strategies the author uses. The Critical Essay questions in the Intermediate 1 exam will often ask you to write about character, and if you go on to sit Intermediate 2 or Higher in future, the essay questions there will mention characterisation.

NOW TRY THIS

Read the following explanations and prompts. Then answer the questions.

1. Sometimes the author **describes the way a character looks**. Look again at the first paragraph of the story. Think about how Lily looks. How do you think the author wants us to feel about Lily? How does the author make us feel this?
2. Sometimes the author **gives the character something to think about**. Look at the first two paragraphs again. What does Lily actually think about? How does Dilys Rose make us feel sorry for her and tell us a little about her character?
3. Sometimes the author **gives the character something to do**. In paragraph 5 we are told that, '*Lily went into the interview room holding out her number.*' Why do you think she does this? What might she be trying to prove? How do you think she is feeling at this point in the story?
4. Sometimes the author **gets a character to speak in a certain way**. Look at paragraphs 12 and 15. How can we tell from Lily's speech that she is Scottish? Now look at paragraph 35. What do the writer's uses of ellipsis (three dots like this …) show us about how Lily is feeling at this point in the story?

5. Sometimes the author **gives us information about the way a character lives**. It gradually becomes clear that Lily is very poor. Look again at paragraphs 1, 26, 28, 30 and 43. Note down all the details that tell us how little money Lily has.

6. Sometimes the author **makes a comment about a character**. Can you find an example of this in paragraph 21? If this comment is true about Lily, how will it affect her chance of getting the new house she wants for herself and her son?

7. Sometimes the author **makes one character say something about another character**. Lily speaks quite a lot in the story about her son Sammy. Have a look though at paragraph 37. Which other character does she speak about? What does she say about him? What does this show about the kind of person Lily is?

8. Sometimes an author **gives a character mixed feelings**. You should know the whole story quite well by now. Lily seems to have two main feelings about the clerk. One feeling is based on his job, one is based on him as a person. What do you think these feelings are?

9. Sometimes an author **gets a character to come to a decision**. What does Lily decide to do at the end of the story? Why do you think she decides this?

NOW TRY THIS

Now that you have thought in detail about Lily, brainstorm as many words as you can think of to describe her.

Let's think more closely about that decision that Lily makes. At the end of the story it's quite clear that she is at least planning to try to destroy her flat in a fire so that the council will be forced to re-house her. Rose does not tell us this outright, nor does she have Lily suddenly think, 'I know, I'll burn the flat down and then they'll have to move me!' Rose uses **implication**. This means that she suggests things to us by giving clues rather than telling us outright.

NOW TRY THIS

Read the ending of the story, from paragraph 40 onwards. From these paragraphs, pick out quotations that suggest what Lily is about to do, and show how these words help us to work out her plan. Set out your answers in a table like the one below. The first one has been done for you.

Quotation	How this suggests what Lily will do
'A piece of broken bottle had trapped the sun on its curve and shone fiercely. A wisp of smoke curled round the jagged edge. Below the glass, the weeds were scorched.' (paragraph 40)	Lily notices how easily a fire can start.

Complete the table in your notebook.

When Lily makes the plan she is absolutely desperate. She clearly feels that the council will not help her. By this point she's not really able to think straight. However, we can examine her plan more clearly.

NOW TRY THIS

Discuss the following questions in pairs or groups. You should be able to find several answers for each question.

1.   How could she benefit from carrying out this plan?
2.   What are the risks involved in this plan?
3.   Which parts of her life could actually be made worse by her carrying out her plan?
4.   Which bad parts of her life still won't get any better even if her plan works?
5.   If she changes her mind and doesn't burn the flat down, what do you think will happen to her?
6.   Do you think she should do what she plans? If not, what do you think she should do instead? How else could she realistically try to move house?
7.   Did you find the ending of the story convincing and satisfying? What was good about the way the story ended? Was there anything you disliked about the ending?

Setting

The Easter Drumbeath estate is the most important setting in the story. Lily and the clerk discuss it, and she often thinks about it, although she does not actually go back there until the very end of the story. Lily's character has been very much shaped by the setting she lives in, and her desperate decision at the end is a way of trying to escape from it. The other settings in the story are important too, and are almost all used to build up Lily's feelings of depression and powerlessness.

NOW TRY THIS

Look again at the second and third paragraphs of the story. Which three place settings are mentioned? How does the writer make each one sound unpleasant? Set out your answers in a table like the one below.

Setting	How it is made to sound unpleasant
1	
2	
3	

NOW TRY THIS

Look at paragraph 4. The author is creating a **contrast** (a difference) between the setting on the poster and the environment that Lily is used to in Easter Drumbeath. Pick out the details that make this contrast. The first one has been done as an example.

The poster	Easter Drumbeath
'very green grass'	Lily has never seen such green grass

In paragraph 4, Rose also uses a technique called **personification**. She makes the litter in Drumbeath seem as if it is alive.

NOW TRY THIS

Which two verbs personify the litter?

While Lily is with the clerk, she constantly thinks about the estate, as well as speaking to him about it. For example the '*dull*' green form the clerk pulls out in paragraph 11 reminds her of the colour of the flat doors. There's another contrast at work here, because the last time we read about something green in the story it wasn't a dull door, but the bright grass on the poster in the waiting room. The door is real, though the poster is only imaginary.

NOW TRY THIS

Look at paragraph 11. Explain why the name of Lily's street is inappropriate.

After she leaves the council office, Lily walks home. The first part of her walk takes her into much nicer surroundings. We are told that the walkway by the canal is '*landscaped*' (paragraph 40), which suggests that someone has taken the trouble to create it, and to care for it, as a nice place for people to go walking.

NOW TRY THIS

Look at paragraph 40. Lily briefly finds herself in nicer surroundings. Quote the sentence that captures her only pleasant moment in the entire story.

As her walk progresses, however, Lily heads back towards a more familiar and nastier setting. We are told that:

> 'Towards the end of the landscaped walkway, she began to start noticing the litter.' (paragraph 40)

Someone has clearly once tried to make a clear divide between these contrasting settings because Lily climbs through a

> 'torn fence'

in paragraph 41. As she passes through the fence she notices that she's come to end of

> 'the neat bungalows and their well-tended lawns,'

and that the birds don't sing on her estate.

We never actually see Lily in her own flat. The story only takes her as far as the shop.

NOW TRY THIS

Look at paragraphs 43 and 44. Make a list of all the ways in which the writer makes the shop seem very unpleasant. It will help if you think about the shopkeeper, and about the things he has to sell, as well as just thinking about the shop itself.

Although we don't follow Lily right home, there has been a lot of detail earlier in the story about what her flat is like.

NOW TRY THIS

Read back over Lily's interview with the clerk. Pick out as many details as you can to show what Lily's flat is like. Make a list of them in your notebook.

Word choice

To finish off our work on this story, we are going to look at some smaller details of word choice and other techniques that Rose uses.

First we are going to think about the other people who are in the waiting room, and who go in to see the clerk just before Lily does. (You'll find this couple in paragraphs 3 and 5.)

NOW TRY THIS

Answer these questions.

1. Which words or phrases in these paragraphs tell us that although the woman is 'thin' the man is large or fat?
2. Which words or phrases in these paragraphs tell us that the man is in a bad mood even *before* he goes in for the interview?
3. Which words or phrases in these paragraphs tell us that both the people are in a bad mood *after* the interview?

The author of this story chooses her words very carefully.

4. Which word in paragraph 2 is meant to intrigue or puzzle you and make you read on?

Because the whole story is told from Lily's **point of view**, we often get a chance to overhear her thoughts. There is one point in the story, however, when those thoughts, or at least the words she thinks them in, are not entirely her own.

NOW TRY THIS

Read paragraph 2 again. Make a list of all the words or phrases that sound as if they were originally said to Lily by staff at the hospital.

Look at this quotation from paragraph 32:

> 'It was as if the two of them were playing a strange game of Snakes and Ladders, with Lily landing on more than her fair share of snakes'.

Now read paragraphs 30 to 32.

NOW TRY THIS

Explain what the above quotation means. What are the snakes? What are the ladders?

Here is another example of **implication** from paragraph 37:

> 'Mr Martin, from flat eleven, hanging from a rope, poor man. There were ... things moving all over him.'

NOW TRY THIS

Answer these questions:

1. What **exactly** did Sammy see?
2. Why can't Lily say what the '*things*' were?

Theme

The theme of a story (or of a novel, play, film or poem) is the big idea behind it. The theme is something the writer wants you to think about or learn about. It may be an idea the writer is trying to explore. A theme should be something that you can express using just one or two simple words.

The theme should be something that you can imagine fitting another story (or novel, or play, or film, or poem) too – it should not just be specific to the text you have just read. For example, although the subject of *EastEnders* is the lives of a group of people who live and work around Albert Square in Walford, and the subject of *Coronation Street* is the lives of the people who live and work around the street with that name in Weatherfield, the theme of both these programmes, and of all 'soaps', is community. The theme of *Romeo and Juliet* is love, but that's one of the themes of *Shrek*, too! Another theme of *Shrek* is how society treats someone who looks very different. In the case of *Shrek*, the different character is a stinky green ogre, but the same theme could fit any text where the character is different because of their age, their skin colour, or a disability.

NOW TRY THIS

Finally, ask yourself what the theme(s) of *Snakes and Ladders* is/are. What did the writer want you to think about or learn about? Give details from the story to prove the theme(s).

Essay writing

In Chapter 9 you will learn how to write Intermediate 1 Critical Essays. Although the advice in that chapter is general, and will help you to write all your Critical Essays, the examples in that chapter are based on *Snakes and Ladders* and on the work we've done on this story.

You might want to go to that chapter now and work through it to write your first literature essay.

Possible essay choices

Once you have studied Chapter 9, on essay writing, you might like to try one of these essays, which are also suitable for *Snakes and Ladders*.

Above the prose essay choices on the exam paper you'll see the following words:

> **Answers to questions in this section should refer to such relevant features as: content, character, theme, imagery…**

Now look at the essay choices:

- Choose a novel or a short story in which one of the main characters has to make a decision.

  Explain what that decision is and show why it is an important one.

or

- Choose a novel or a short story which has a surprise ending.

  Briefly say what happens in the story and then go on to say why the surprise ending made a good finish to the story.

4

Prose: Kid In A Bin

GETTING IN

We're about to read a short story in which unusual things happen in a very familiar setting. The whole story takes place in a McDonald's.

Before you read the story, discuss the following questions with a partner, small group or your class.

- What kind of people would you expect to find in a McDonald's?

- What sorts of things would be happening there on a typical day?

FIRST THOUGHTS

As you read through the story for the first time, think about the answers to these questions.

- Who is the main character of this story?

- Where does he live?

- What has happened in this person's family life?

- Why has he chosen to live where he does?

Kid in a Bin

1. From opening till closing time, Anthony lives inside the wooden flip-top rubbish container which houses the plastic rubbish bags at McDonald's. His skin has become whiter and his brown hair is long and greasy; his eyes are cat-sharp. He is a bit over a metre tall which allows him to stand inside the bin. In the mornings there is plenty of room for him to stretch, scratch, turn around or even curl up and doze. By afternoon the empty foam cartons of Big Macs and cheeseburgers and McFeasts swell the plastic bag and choke out the light and space, forcing him either to stand thin against the back wall or lean into the rubbish, until one of the counter crew changes the bag.

2. At different times, Anthony touches his finger against the inside of the used chicken containers which are made of cardboard and have a small piece of tissue paper where salt sticks to the splotches of grease. Old men use the most salt, followed by boys, girls, older women and younger men. The most users are younger men. The least users are younger women – about the age of Miss Tomagin, Anthony's third class teacher, last year. By licking the salt stuck to his fingers, Anthony guesses the age and sex of the chicken-eaters. When the cartons come through the flip-top bin, he touches, tastes and guesses the owners before they reach the exit door. Anthony likes to watch the customers. For a really good look he waits for the flip-top lid to be pushed inwards by a depositor, otherwise he has to be content with one horizontal slit and two perpendicular ones about a centimetre wide surrounding the lid. Anthony's world comes in slices.

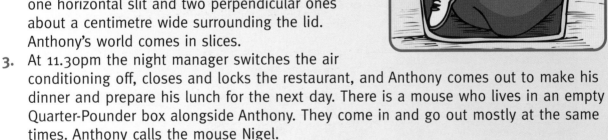

3. At 11.30pm the night manager switches the air conditioning off, closes and locks the restaurant, and Anthony comes out to make his dinner and prepare his lunch for the next day. There is a mouse who lives in an empty Quarter-Pounder box alongside Anthony. They come in and go out mostly at the same times. Anthony calls the mouse Nigel.

4. It is Sunday, 11.40am. Outside the wind spits needles of rain. The customers are bursting through the doors, shaking like washed dogs, and laughing. Anthony is almost asleep in his bin – the air is humid and smells of sodden shoes and wet hair. Outside his bin is a boy exactly the same height as Anthony. The boy sees Anthony's eyes as he pushes his tray of rubbish through the swing-top. He pushes the flap again and Anthony ducks down inside. He is too late, the boy sees his head disappearing behind the garbage. The boy pushes the flap once more and then reaches his arm in as far as he can in the direction of

Anthony's disappearing head. His arm is too short to reach Anthony. The boy's mother sees what he's doing and shrieks at him to get his hand out of the filth.

5. The boy goes to his mother. 'There's a kid in there.'

6. 'Sit down, or I'll slap you.'

7. 'There's a kid in the rubbish box, I saw his head.'

8. 'Wait here, I'll get you another coke.'

9. The boy waits for his mother to reach the counter and then goes back to the bin. 'Hey you in there.' He tries to see inside by holding the flap open. 'What are you doing in there? You're not allowed in there.' A group of high school girls are giggling and nudging each other to have a look at the boy talking to the rubbish box. 'Why don't you come outside?' the boy says. The high school girls splutter into their thick shakes. The boy's mother returns with the drink which she decides to give him in the car.

10. 'It's probably a cardboard clown, or something,' she says.

11. 'No it isn't, it's got real hair and real eyes, and it moves.' The mother sees the high school girls looking at her and drags the boy out into the rain.

12. Inside the bin, Anthony eats one of the three Junior Burgers he prepared the night before. He watches the boy being dragged to the door, and the coke being spilled as the boy looks and points back towards him. Anthony eats very slowly. Nigel is not in sight but Anthony pulls off a thumb-sized chunk of bun and places it in his box.

13. A newspaper comes through the flap and Anthony rescues it, saving it for later when the shop is empty. Almost every day something to read comes in his bin. He has a small collection of torn-out newspaper items and one colour magazine article which has a picture of him, his mother and father and his sister. The newspaper ones have

pictures of him alone. He carries them all in the pocket of his jeans, which are so tight that he has long since stopped doing up the top stud. The newspaper cuttings have begun to crack and split along the crease lines, from repeated opening and folding with greasy fingers. The magazine article is his favourite. Throughout stretching days in the dark bin, he feels the wad squeezed into his pocket, waiting for the eaters to go and the noise to stop. On wet nights the closing of the store takes longer. The floor is washed twice by tired counter crew whose lips press together and whose name tags flop in time with the swing and pull of the mops.

14. Anthony listens for the sequence; air conditioner shut down, lights out, door lock click, and total quiet, except for the refrigerators humming downstairs. He waits several minutes in case the night manager has forgotten something and because he likes to anticipate the coming pleasure. He opens the hinged side panel of the bin from where the rubbish bags are removed and steps out into the customer area. The space rushes at him. Anthony closes his eyes for a moment and then slowly opens them.

15. His legs and back are stiff and tight. He sits at a side booth made of blue plastic and watches Nigel run to the kitchen. It is still raining outside, he can see the drizzle sliding down the outer windows. With just the dull security lights on, he can see no further than the glass boundaries of the store. Once, earlier on, he attempted to look further by cupping his hands against the window and pressing his face against the pane, but all he could see was black, with some tiny lights too far off to matter, and some moths beating against the car-park lights.

16. He goes to the men's toilet, switches on the light and empties his bladder into the stainless steel urinal. He washes his face and moves it from side to side in front of the hot-air drier. Holding his hair back, he inspects his face reflected in the mirror. There is a tiny freckle-like spot on the bony bump of his nose which he feels gently with his fingers, screwing up his eyes for a closer evaluation. The remaining skin is the white of his mother's scone mixture before it was cut into circles with a tumbler and shoved into the oven. Anthony leaves the toilet and goes into the kitchen. From the undercounter refrigerator he takes two containers of orange juice. He switches on the griddle and the French fry vat and sits at the booth near the security light. From his pocket he pulls out the newspaper and magazine articles. He opens them carefully, bending the folds backwards and pressing them into flatness on the table top. With his fingernail he levers up the edge of the foil top sealing the orange juice and tears it away; some drops spill on the newspaper. He brushes them away with his sleeve and reads again under his photograph, with his finger sliding along beneath the words.

EIGHT-YEAR-OLD BOY STILL MISSING

The search continues for eight-year-old Anthony O'Neal who disappeared from his home on August 9th. A police task force has interviewed Anthony's school classmates, neighbours and relatives with no leads to the missing boy's whereabouts. Anthony's mother…

---

17. The griddle is hot and it is time to cook. Anthony stops reading and folds the article back into his pocket. Outside he can hear the rain spatting at the glass, and the trucks changing gear in the distance. Nigel is running underneath the tables.

18. Anthony leans against the rubbish bag; he wants to go to the toilet and regrets drinking too much orange juice in the night. He concentrates on the customers through the slits. A tall lady with six children has come to have a birthday party. The children put on cardboard hats and make noises with balloons; one of them squeals every time the others take their attention from him – he is the birthday boy who shouts at his mother when he spills his thick shake across the table. His mother mops at it with table napkins and tells them he can have another one. He throws a piece of lettuce at the child opposite him who has turned his head away.

19. At the table alongside the birthday party sit a man and a girl. They are not talking. The girl has her back to Anthony and eats her chips one at a time and licks her fingers after each one. The man reads the *Saturday Morning Herald* and Anthony can see only the backs of his hands and the top of his head. As the man lowers his paper to talk to the girl, Anthony wets himself. It is his father, except that he looks older and his skin looks greyer. The girl is his sister, Meredith. Anthony feels for used paper napkins in the garbage. He finds some and attempts to blot up the urine before it leaks under the wooden bin and out onto the customer area. Some of it escapes and sneaks across the floor under the seat of the birthday boy.

20. Anthony presses his eye up against the horizontal slit. It is his father. Meredith appears to be bigger than he remembers. The floor crew supervisor discovers the leaking bin and dispatches a mopper to fix it. Anthony wriggles around the other side of the bin to avoid detection when the side panel is opened. There is something he wishes to tell his father. A message he wants to pass on to both of them. He takes an unused napkin from the bin and feels around until he locates a sundae container with some chocolate flavouring still in the bottom. He dips his forefinger into the container and prints his message in chocolate letters across the napkin delicately, careful not to smear the sauce all over the paper; he places it in an empty Big Mac Box and watches through the crack. When everyone in the customer area is looking at something other than his bin, Anthony flicks the Big Mac Box through the swinging flap and onto his father's table. Meredith jumps and showers chips over her father's paper.

21. 'Someone threw a Big Mac at me,' she says.

22. 'What?' Her father puts down his paper and collects the loose chips.

23. 'Someone threw this at me,' she says again, picking up the box and looking towards the birthday party group. She opens the box and takes out the napkin unfolding it carefully. She wrinkles her face at the chocolate sauce.

24. 'Throw it in the bin, Meredith,' he says.

25. 'It says words, Daddy.'

26. 'What do you mean?'

27. 'The chocolate says words.'

28. 'Let me see.' He reaches for the napkin. 'It does too.'
29. 'What does it say?'
30. 'It says, "STAY ... OUT ... OF ... THE something ... STAY OUT OF THE ... SUN." '
31. 'What does that mean, Daddy?'
32. 'I don't know.' The man's face looks puzzled. He stares at the birthday party group for a long time. There is no one else close enough to have thrown a box onto their table. He places the napkin and the box and the stray chips onto the tray and goes to Anthony's bin. He tilts the opening flap and tips the tray's contents in. Anthony has a close-up flash-view of his father's face. He sees the same ache as he sees in the men's toilet mirror. He watches his father and sister disappear through the exit door.
33. And the days and nights pass. Anthony's father and sister do not come into the restaurant again. Nigel becomes sick from eating rat poison and a lot of his hair falls out. Anthony drinks less orange juice and keeps checking his face in the toilet mirror. He cuts his hair with scissors from the manager's office. One night the manager comes back an hour after closing. Anthony is in the toilet. He switches the light off and hangs onto the clothes hook behind the door of the second toilet cubicle. The manager goes into his office. Anthony waits behind the door. There is a new message written on the back of the toilet door. He has not seen this one before; it says, 'Flush twice – the kitchen is a long way off.' Anthony does not understand the message. If the manager comes into the toilet, Anthony will lift his feet off the ground by holding onto the clothes hook. There is no sound coming from the manager's office. Anthony waits. He thinks of being inside his bin curled up against the fat of the plastic garbage bag, with the murmur of customers and FM music filtering through – impregnable. The fear of being discovered outside his shell is worse than nakedness – worse than peeling the rind off his sanctuary.
34. Anthony feels something brush against his ankle. In the darkness, his eyes search for movement. It is a large tom cat. The manager has brought his cat to hunt for Nigel. Anthony thinks Nigel will die quickly this way. He kicks the cat in the stomach, anyway. It hisses and runs out of the toilet.

35. Within an hour the manager is gone. The restaurant is safe again and Anthony prepares his next day's lunch. He sees Nigel run into the kitchen and he smiles about the big cat. Waiting for the oil to heat, he spreads his collected articles on a table top. He smoothes the magazine one, and looks at the picture of his family. He remembers when it was taken on Meredith's fifth birthday. She got a bicycle with trainer wheels and it was in the background of the photograph. Anthony remembers giving her a large hazelnut chocolate which got left in the sun and which stuck to the foil and would only bend and stretch, rather than snap off in pieces.
36. Where the paper has been creased, some of the letters of the words have come away but this does not disturb Anthony; he has memorised most of them. He slides his

finger under the words beneath the picture of his family. He reads aloud as he was taught in school, and sounds out the difficult words which, like many messages to Anthony, don't make much sense.

Missing school boy Anthony O'Neal, pictured here with his parents and sister, Meredith, was last seen at his home on August 9th. Police believe his disappearance may be related to the death of his mother six weeks earlier. Mrs O'Neal died of metastasic melanoma, of which she was diagnosed six months previously. (Malignant melanoma is a virulent form of skin cancer caused in most cases by exposure of skin to the sun.) A large number of reported sightings of Anthony have been investigated by the police, with no success to date. Fears for the boy's safety have increased as no indication of…

37. The griddle is hot and it is time to cook.
38. Anthony peers out through the horizontal slit in the bin. It is cold outside and the faces of the seated customers go pink around the cheekbones from the warm McDonald's air. The rubbish comes in, tipped from its plastic trays. Anthony waits with Nigel for the store to close.

Robert Carter

THINKING THROUGH

First, share your answers to the 'First Thoughts' questions you were given at the start of the story. Then work out the answers to the following questions:

- Why do you think Anthony behaves the way he does when he sees his father and sister?

- Why doesn't he want to go home with them?

- Why does he send the message he sends?

LET'S GET TO WORK

McDonald's is a familiar setting but the very first sentence of the story makes it clear that weird things are happening there. The author takes a normal setting – a fast food restaurant – and uses it abnormally by making it Anthony's home. As we study this story we'll look especially at how his strange life there begins to seem normal. We'll also examine the different sorts of families in the story.

The author's use of implication

Before we examine Anthony's life in the bin, let's look at his reason for being there. You worked out in the '**First Thoughts**' questions that Anthony has run away from home following the death of his mother. Right at the end of the story we are told what caused her death:

> 'Mrs O'Neal died of metastasic melanoma, of which she was diagnosed six months previously. (Malignant melanoma is a virulent form of skin cancer caused in most cases by exposure of skin to the sun.)'

Before we are told this we are given clues that help us to begin to work at least some of it out. Carter is using **implication**, the skill of suggesting things without telling us them outright.

NOW TRY THIS

Each of the following pieces of evidence from the story hints to us about Anthony's mother. Some of them hint that she has died, others begin to suggest what might have caused her death. Copy and complete the table.

Evidence	What this implies about Anthony's mother
The pictures in the magazine articles have his mother in them, but in the newspaper pictures Anthony is alone. (para 13)	The contrast between the two sorts of pictures suggests to us that Anthony's mother used to be around but now is gone.
He remembers how white his mother's scone mixture was before it got put in the oven. (para 16)	
The news article is suddenly interrupted after the words, 'Anthony's mother ...' (para 16)	

Anthony obviously knows that the doctors think his mother's illness may have been caused by exposure to the sun. He's picked himself a very sun-proof place to hide.

NOW TRY THIS

Re-read the part of the story where his father and sister come into the restaurant (paragraphs 20–32). Write a few sentences to explain how we can tell that Anthony is still very afraid of the sun and its power.

How Anthony's life in the bin is made to seem normal

Because the writers of short stories do not have much length to work with, it's important that they grab the reader's attention straight away. The first sentence of this story certainly does that:

> **'From opening till closing time, Anthony lives inside the wooden flip-top rubbish container which houses the plastic rubbish bags at McDonald's.'**

We immediately want to know who Anthony is, why he lives in the bin, and how he manages to do so without being caught. The bizarre situation engages our interest.

However, the longer the story goes on, the more Anthony's life in the bin seems normal. This doesn't mean that we begin to think it is a good way for people in general to live, but that it starts to seem normal and unsurprising for Anthony to live this way.

One way Anthony's life in the bin is made to seem normal is through the author's **choice of tense**.

NOW TRY THIS

Answer the following questions:

1. Look again at the story. Which tense is it written in?
2. Now, even if you haven't studied them, take a quick look at the two other stories in this book, *Lamb to the Slaughter* (pages 113–122) and *Snakes and Ladders* (pages 69–73). Which tense is used in these two stories?

Robert Carter, who wrote *Kid in a Bin*, has deliberately chosen to use a tense that is not often used for writing prose fiction. Now answer this question:

3. How does using this particular tense help to make Anthony's life in the bin seem normal?

Another way in which such a strange life starts to seem normal is that **the writer gives us a sense of time passing**. The longer Anthony lives in the bin, the more natural it seems that he will keep on living there.

NOW TRY THIS

We can tell that time is passing because Anthony is growing and changing. Copy and complete the table.

Paragraph	Evidence	How we know time is passing
1	'His skin has become whiter'	He must have been indoors for a long time away from the sun
1	'his brown hair is long and greasy'	
13	'his jeans, which are so tight he has long ago stopped doing up the top stud'	
13	'The newspaper cuttings have begun to crack and split along the crease lines'	
16	'There is a tiny freckle-like spot on the bony bump of his nose'	
33	'Nigel becomes sick from eating rat poison and a lot of his hair falls out'	

We can also tell that Anthony has been there for a long time, and that McDonald's has become his whole 'world', because **he understands so well how the restaurant's customers behave**.

NOW TRY THIS

Read paragraph 2 again. Copy and complete the following paragraph:

Anthony has spent so long living in McDonald's that he now understands how certain customers behave. He knows how much _____ each type of _____ uses. Anthony tests the cardboard _____ _____ that he finds in his bin. He _____ them with his _____ and then licks to see how _____ salt they leave behind. The people who use _____ salt are old _____. The ones who use _____ are younger _____. He _____ the salt and guesses the _____ before they reach the _____ _____.

The fact that he understands the customers' behaviour so well shows us how long Anthony has been living in McDonald's.

Carter also makes the boy's life in the bin seem normal by showing us that Anthony has a **routine**, and that McDonald's itself runs by following a routine. There are certain things that Anthony does every day, and there are certain things that happen in McDonald's every day

NOW TRY THIS

Let's begin by looking at Anthony's routine. Answer the following questions:

1. Quote the words from paragraph 1 that tell us which part of the day Anthony spends inside the bin.
2. Look at paragraph 3. What does Anthony do at 11.30 each night?
3. According to paragraph 3, who else comes and goes at the same time as Anthony?
4. Look at paragraph 14. Explain the two reasons why Anthony always waits for a few minutes before leaving the bin at night.
5. Read paragraph 16. Where does Anthony go first after leaving the bin?
6. Read paragraphs 12 and 16. What does Anthony eat and drink each day?
7. Read paragraphs 19 and 33. Which detail of his routine does Anthony change? Why does he change it?

Of course if he wants to avoid being caught, Anthony has to make sure that the routines and habits of his life fit round the routine of the day in McDonald's. He needs to understand how the restaurant day runs so that he is active only when the staff and customers are away.

NOW TRY THIS

Answer the following questions about McDonald's routine:

1. Look at paragraph 1. What happens at McDonald's by the start of every afternoon?
2. Look at paragraph 2. What kind of container is always used for chicken portions?
3. Look at paragraph 3. What happens at 11.30 each night?
4. Look at paragraph 13. How does the store routine vary on wet days?
5. Look at paragraph 20. What happens whenever liquid is noticed on the floor?

Anthony must be lonely living in his bin. Not only is he cut off from his family, and presumably mourning his mother, but he has no contact with any other human beings at all. He sees people all day but never speaks to any of them. He loves watching people, but he doesn't dare communicate with them. Maybe that's why one thing he does which is quite normal for a boy his age is that **he has a pet**.

93

It's quite common for an eight-year-old boy to have a pet. There's nothing unusual about having a mouse either. Anthony looks after his pet well, makes sure he gives it food, and tries to protect it from the cat. All of this is quite ordinary behaviour. The one unusual thing is that he calls the mouse Nigel.

NOW TRY THIS

Answer these questions:

1. What's unusual about calling a pet mouse Nigel?
2. Why do you think he chose this name for the mouse?

Carter, the author, does not try to make us think that McDonald's is perfect. We've already seen some of the changes in Anthony since he began to live there. We are aware that he has put on weight, that he has a spot on his nose, and that his hair is greasy. This might all be there to suggest that his diet of nothing but McDonald's food is actually not very good for him. (A documentary movie called *Super Size Me*, which came out in 2004, suggested this more strongly. A journalist, Morgan Spurlock, decided that for one month he would only eat and drink McDonald's products. Over that time he gained a huge amount of weight and severely affected his own health and fitness.)

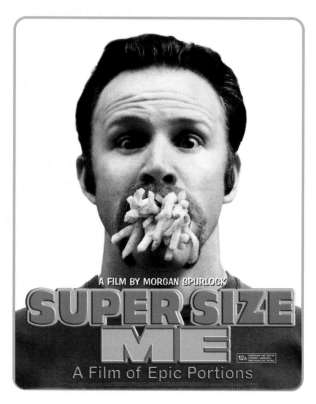

Carter also suggests that McDonald's isn't that wonderful when he shows us the graffiti on the toilet wall.

NOW TRY THIS

Read paragraph 33 again. Anthony notices some new graffiti. The customer who wrote it is suggesting something very rude about the food there.

■   What is the customer trying to say about McDonald's food?

So we have a story in which we know that the setting, McDonald's, is not a perfect place. However, another way in which it is made to seem like a normal, or even safe, place for Anthony to live at the moment is that **the outside world is made to seem like an unpleasant place**.

Quite often Carter gives this impression by using the **weather**. For example, look at the opening of paragraph 4. The wind is made to seem alive and violent when we are told that it:

> 'spits needles of rain'.

When a writer takes something like the wind, which is not alive, and describes it to make it seem as if it is alive, this is called **personification**. Making the weather vicious like this makes the outside world seem like a dangerous and scary place to be.

In the next sentence we are told that:

> 'The customers are bursting through the doors, shaking like washed dogs, and laughing.'

The use of the word '*laughing*' suggests that coming in to McDonald's immediately makes people feel happier.

Even at night, when the restaurant is empty except for Anthony, we are still given the impression that the outside world is quite a bleak place. In paragraph 15 we are told:

> 'It is still raining outside, he can see the drizzle sliding down the outer windows.'

Although Anthony here tries to look outside, the world out there seems rather unreal compared with the humming refrigerators and blue plastic booths of the McDonald's. We are told:

'Once earlier on, he attempted to look further by cupping his hands against the window and pressing his face against the pane, but all he could see was black, with some tiny lights too far off to matter, and some moths beating against the car-park lights.'

Of course one other reason why the outside world is such an unpleasant and frightening place is because of what it did to his mother. We know already that Anthony blames the sun for her death, and that he wants his father and sister to stay out of sunlight. His chosen home in the bin keeps him away from that same scary sun.

The author does even more than show us that it is normal for Anthony to live this way. We can see by the end of the story that Anthony would be terrified to live anywhere else.

NOW TRY THIS

Read paragraph 33 again. Which sentence tells us that Anthony would hate to be caught and sent home?

The portrayal of families in the story

The main focus of the story is on Anthony, and on the weird life he's chosen to live after a tragedy in his own family. However, the story features two other families too. The first of these other families appears in paragraphs 4 to 11. The second one can be found in paragraph 18.

You might think that Anthony's family life is about as odd as it could be. After all, his mother is dead and he has run away from home at a very young age without being caught and has come to live in a bin. However, there are a number of ways in which Anthony's family is deliberately made to seem very much like the other two families in the story.

Both families, like Anthony's, have a young boy in them. In fact when we meet the family in paragraphs 4 to 11 we are clearly told that the boy is:

'exactly the same height as Anthony'

The writer points out how alike Anthony and the other boy are.

The centre of attention of the other family is:

'the birthday boy'

Another similarity between Anthony's family and the others we see is that each family is only shown with one parent. In Anthony's family only his father is left, while in the other two families we only see the mothers.

Robert Carter could have shown lots of different sorts of families coming into the restaurant. He could have put happy families with two parents in the story and shown us Anthony feeling jealous. There must be a deliberate reason why Carter has used families which are in some ways similar to Anthony's.

NOW TRY THIS

Read the paragraphs in which the other families are mentioned. As you read, build up two lists of information. Lay it out in a table like the one below. The first details have been done for you.

What makes these families seem unhappy

Paragraphs 4 to 11	Paragraph 18
The little boy's mother *'shrieks'* at him	The birthday boy *'squeals'* to get other people's attention

See how many more you can find.

NOW TRY THIS

Answer these questions:

1. What do you think the author wants to say about family life in general?
2. Why do you think he does not put any happy families in the story?

The language of the story

Carter uses a number of language techniques as he tells his story. We are going to look especially at his use of **repetition**, and his use of a **symbol**.

Repetition means using a word or a phrase more than once. When we talk about a writer using repetition we mean that he or she **deliberately** repeats a word or a phrase so that it is used **more often than you would expect**.

NOW TRY THIS

There is one particular sentence which comes up twice in the story:

'The griddle is hot and it is time to cook.'

Answer the following questions:

1. In which two paragraphs do we find this sentence?
2. What is always happening in the story just before this sentence appears?

When we find an example of this kind of repetition, it begins to let us know what is important to the writer, or perhaps to a character in the text. It's time to work out why you think the writer chose to repeat this sentence:

3. What do you think he is trying to say about Anthony's feelings?
4. What do you think he is trying to say about Anthony's life?
5. Why does he use this sentence at these points in the story?

A **symbol** is an object or a picture which stands for something else, often something very important. When we see the symbol, we think of the idea or the feeling that it stands for.

NOW TRY THIS

What do the following symbols stand for?

Some symbols give us information.

What does it mean if you see this symbol on any food that you buy?

What does it mean if you see this symbol on the label of a piece of clothing?

One symbolic object in this story is the chocolate Anthony gave to Meredith on her fifth birthday.

'Anthony remembers giving her a large hazelnut chocolate which got left in the sun and which stuck to the foil and would only bend and stretch, rather than snap off in pieces.'

Like Anthony's mother, this chocolate is damaged by the sun. The connection with Anthony's mother makes this chocolate an important and symbolic object.

NOW TRY THIS

Copy and complete the mind map to explain how the chocolate stands for different themes and emotions in the story.

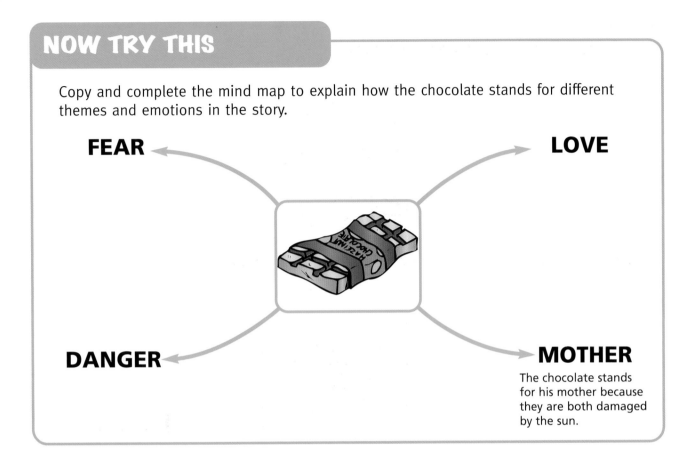

FEAR

LOVE

DANGER

MOTHER
The chocolate stands for his mother because they are both damaged by the sun.

The ending

The last line of the story is:

'Anthony waits with Nigel for the store to close.'

If you've read them, think about the other stories in this book. Mary's life changes hugely over the evening covered in the story *Lamb to the Slaughter*. At the end of *Snakes and Ladders* Lily seems about to do something huge and drastic because she wants to change her life. This story is quite unusual. Nothing has changed. Anthony is left there, still in McDonald's, still following his daily routine.

NOW TRY THIS

Answer the following questions. You may want to discuss them with a partner, a group, or the class.

1. Do you like the way the story ends?
2. Why do you feel this way about the ending?
3. Why do you think the author chose to give the story this sort of ending?

Now think about Anthony's life after the story has ended. Again you may wish to discuss the answers for these questions with a partner, a group, or the class.

4. Where do you think Anthony will be living a year after the end of the story?
5. Do you think he will ever be caught? If so, what will happen to cause his discovery?
6. What do you think will happen to him if he is found living in McDonald's?
7. Do you think there is any chance of him ever going back to his family?
8. What difficulties would he face if he tried to live at home again with his father and Meredith?

NOW TRY THIS

There's one final question for you to answer about this story. There isn't a right or wrong answer for this one, because the story doesn't give enough evidence for us to know the answer. However, now that you have studied the story in depth you should be able to come up with an answer.

Think of an answer for the question below. Share your answer with the rest of the class. Make a list of all the answers that people think are possible.

We know why Anthony ran away from home. We know why he is hiding in the dark, but we don't know this:

■ Why do you think Anthony chose to live **exactly** where he does: in a bin in McDonald's. Why did he choose **that particular place?**

Possible essay tasks

Now that you've finished studying this story, you could tackle the following essay questions. Remember to follow the advice from Chapter 9 on how to write literature essays.

Above the prose essay choices on the exam paper you'll see the following words:

> **Answers to questions in this section should refer to such relevant features as: content, character, theme, imagery…**

Now look at the essay choices:

■ Choose a short story which interested you because it deals with a child or a young person.

Say what happens to the child or young person and how the writer helps you understand the situation the young person is in.

or

■ Choose a short story which makes you sad.

Briefly describe what happens in the story and go on to show how the story made you feel this way.

5

Prose: Lamb To The Slaughter

 GETTING IN

We're about to read a short story by Roald Dahl. When you were younger you might have read some of the books he wrote for children, or you may have seen some of the films based on these books. He wrote *Charlie and the Chocolate Factory*, *Matilda*, *The Witches*, *James and the Giant Peach*, *George's Marvellous Medicine*, *The Twits* and many other books. You may not know that Dahl also wrote stories for adults. Many of these stories involve crimes. Often his criminals are people who at first seem quite harmless.

Before you read the story, discuss this issue with a partner, a group or your class. What is your mental image of a typical murderer? For example:

1. Is a typical murderer male or female?

2. How old would this person be?

3. What weapon would they use?

4. Why would this person commit murder?

5. Who might their typical victim be?

6. What kind of place would the murderer live in?

7. What would a typical murderer's job be?

8. Is it likely or unlikely that the murderer would get caught?

Share and discuss your answers.

FIRST THOUGHTS

As you read through the story for the first time, think about the answers to these questions. They are pretty similar to the ones above:

1. Who is the murderer in this story?

2. How old do you think this person is?

3. What weapon does the killer use?

4. Why does this person commit murder?

5. Who is the victim?

6. What kind of place does the killer live in?

7. What is the killer's job?

8. Does it seem that the murderer will be caught?

Lamb to the Slaughter

1. The room was warm and clean, the curtains drawn, the two table lamps alight – hers and the one by the empty chair opposite. On the sideboard behind her, two tall glasses, soda water, whiskey. Fresh ice cubes in the thermos bucket.

2. Mary Maloney was waiting for her husband to come home from work.

3. Now and again she would glance up at the clock, but without anxiety, merely to please herself with the thought that each minute gone by made it nearer the time when he would come. There was a slow smiling air about her, and about everything she did. The drop of the head as she bent over her sewing was curiously tranquil. Her skin – for this was her sixth month with child – had acquired a wonderful translucent quality, her mouth was soft, and her eyes with their new placid look seemed larger, darker than before.

4. When the clock said ten minutes to five she began to listen, and a few moments later, punctually as always, she heard the tyres on the gravel outside, the car door slamming, the footsteps passing the window, the key turning in the lock. She laid aside her sewing, stood up, and went forward to kiss him as he came in.

5. 'Hello darling,' she said.

6. 'Hello,' he answered.

7. She took his coat and hung it in the closet. Then she walked over and made the drinks, a strongish one for him, a weak one for herself; and soon she was back again in her chair with the sewing, and he in the other, opposite, holding the tall glass with both hands, rocking it so the ice cubes tinkled against the side.

8. For her this was always a blissful time of day. She knew he didn't want to speak much until the first drink was finished, and she, on her side, was content to sit quietly, enjoying his company after the long hours alone in the house. She loved to luxuriate in the presence of this man, and to feel – almost as a sunbather feels the sun – that warm male glow that came out of him to her when they were alone together. She loved him for the way he sat loosely in a chair, for the way he came in a door, or moved slowly across the room with long strides. She loved the intent, far-away look in his eyes when they rested on her, the funny shape of the mouth. And especially the way he remained silent about his tiredness, sitting still with himself until the whiskey had taken some of it away.

9. 'Tired darling?'

10. 'Yes,' he said. 'I'm tired.' As he spoke, he did an unusual thing. He lifted the glass and drained it in one swallow although there was still half of it, at least half of it, left. She wasn't really watching him but she knew what he had done because she heard the ice cubes falling back against the bottom of the empty glass when he lowered his arm. He paused for a moment leaning forward in the chair, then he got up and went slowly over to fetch himself another.

11. 'I'll get it!' she cried, jumping up.

12. 'Sit down,' he said.

13. When he came back, she noticed that the new drink was dark amber with the quantity of whiskey in it.

14. 'Darling, shall I get your slippers?'

15. 'No.'

16. She watched him as he began to sip the dark yellow drink, and she could see little oily swirls in the liquid because it was so strong.

17. 'I think it's a shame,' she said, 'that when a policeman gets to be as senior as you, they keep him walking about on his feet all day long.'

18. He didn't answer, so she bent her head again and went on again with her sewing; but each time he lifted the drink to his lips, she heard the ice cubes clinking against the side of the glass.

19. 'Darling,' she said. 'Would you like me to get you some cheese? I haven't made any supper because it's Thursday.'

20. 'No,' he said.

21. 'If you're too tired to eat out,' she went on, 'it's still not too late. There's plenty of meat and stuff in the freezer, and you can have it right here and not even move out of the chair.'

22. Her eyes waited on him for an answer, a smile, a little nod, but he made no sign.

23. 'Anyway,' she went on, 'I'll get you some cheese and crackers first.'

24. 'I don't want it,' he said.

25. She moved uneasily in her chair, the large eyes still watching his face. 'But you must have supper. I can easily do it here. I'd like to do it. We can have lamb chops. Or pork. Anything you want. Everything's in the freezer.'

26. 'Forget it,' he said.

27. 'But darling, you must eat! I'll fix it for you anyway, and you can have it or not as you like.'

28. She stood up and placed her sewing on the table by the lamp.

29. 'Sit down,' he said. 'Just for a minute, sit down.'

30. It wasn't until then she began to get frightened.

31. 'Go on,' he said. 'Sit down.'

32. She lowered herself back slowly into the chair, watching him all the time with those large, bewildered eyes. He had finished the second drink and he was staring down into the glass frowning.

33. 'Listen,' he said, 'I've got something to tell you.'

34. 'What is it darling? What's the matter?'

35. He had become absolutely motionless, and he kept his head down so that the light from the lamp beside him fell across the upper part of his face, leaving the chin and mouth in shadow. She noticed there was a little muscle moving near the corner of his left eye.

36. 'This is going to be a bit of a shock to you I'm afraid,' he said. 'But I've thought about it a great deal and I've decided the only thing to do is tell you right away. I hope you won't blame me too much.'

37. And he told her. It didn't take long, four or five minutes at most, and she sat very still through it all, watching him with a kind of dazed horror as he went further and further away from her with each word.

38. 'So there it is,' he added. 'And I know it's kind of a bad time to be telling you, but there simply wasn't any other way. Of course I'll give you money and see you're looked after. But there really needn't be any fuss. I hope not anyway. It wouldn't be good for my job.'

39. Her first instinct was not to believe any of it, to reject it all. It occurred to her that perhaps he hadn't even spoken, that she herself had imagined the whole thing. Maybe if she went about her business and acted as though she hadn't been listening, then later, when she sort of woke up again, she might find none of it had ever happened.

40. 'I'll get the supper,' she managed to whisper, and this time he didn't stop her.

41. When she walked across the room she couldn't feel her feet touching the floor. She couldn't feel anything at all – except a slight nausea and a desire to vomit. Everything was automatic now – down the stairs to the cellar, the light switch, the deep freeze, the hand inside the cabinet taking hold of the first object it met. She lifted it out, and looked at it. It was wrapped in paper, so she took off the paper and looked at it again.

42. A leg of lamb.

43. All right then, they would have lamb for supper. She carried it upstairs, holding the thin bone end of it with both her hands, as she went through the living-room she saw him standing over by the window with his back to her and she stopped.

44. 'For God's sake,' he said hearing her, but not turning round, 'Don't make supper for me. I'm going out.'

45. At that point Mary Maloney simply walked up behind him and without any pause she swung the big frozen leg of lamb high in the air and brought it down as hard as she could on the back of his head.

46. She might just as well have hit him with a steel club.

47. She stepped back a pace waiting, and the funny thing was that he remained standing there for four or five seconds, gently swaying. Then he crashed to the carpet.

48. The violence of the crash, the noise, the small table overturning, helped bring her out of the shock. She came out slowly, feeling cold and surprised, and she stood for a while blinking at the body, still holding the ridiculous piece of meat tight with both hands.

49. All right, she told herself. So I've killed him.

50. It was extraordinary, now, how clear her mind became all of a sudden. She began thinking very fast. As the wife of a detective, she knew quite well what the penalty would be. That was fine. It made no difference to her. In fact it would be a relief. On the other hand, what about the child? What were the laws about murderers with unborn children? Did they kill them both – mother and child? Or did they wait until the tenth month? What did they do?

51. Mary Maloney didn't know. And she certainly wasn't prepared to take a chance.

52. She carried the meat into the kitchen, placed it in a pan, turned the oven on high, and shoved it inside. Then she washed her hands and ran upstairs to the bedroom. She sat down before the mirror, tidied her face, touched up her lips and her face. She tried to smile. It came out rather peculiar. She tried again.

53. 'Hello Sam,' she said brightly, aloud.

54. The voice sounded peculiar too.

55. 'I want some potatoes please, Sam. Yes, and I think a can of peas.'

56. That was better. Both the smile and the voice were coming out better now. She rehearsed it several times more. Then she ran downstairs, took her coat and went out the back door, down the garden and into the street.

57. It wasn't six o'clock yet and the lights were still on in the grocery shop.

58. 'Hello Sam,' she said brightly, smiling at the man behind the counter.

59. 'Why good evening, Mrs. Maloney. How're *you*?'

60. 'I want some potatoes please, Sam. Yes, and I think a can of peas.'

61. The man turned and reached up behind him on the shelf for the peas.

62. 'Patrick decided he's tired and doesn't want to eat out tonight,' she told him. 'We usually go out Thursdays, you know, and now he's caught me without any vegetables in the house.'

63. 'Then how about meat, Mrs. Maloney?'

64. 'No I've got meat, thanks. I got a nice leg of lamb, from the freezer.'

65. 'Oh.'

66. 'I don't much like cooking it frozen, Sam but I'm taking a chance on it this time. You think it will be all right?'

67. 'Personally,' the grocer said, 'I don't believe it makes any difference. You see these Idaho potatoes?'

68. 'Oh yes that'll be fine. Two of those.'

69. 'Anything else?' The grocer cocked his head on one side, looking at her pleasantly. 'How about afterwards? What you going to give him for afterwards?'

70. 'Well – what would you suggest, Sam?'

71. The man glanced around the shop. 'How about a nice big slice of cheesecake? I know he likes that.'

72. 'Perfect,' she said. 'He loves it.'

73. And when it was all wrapped up and she had paid, she put on her brightest smile and said, 'Thank you, Sam. Good night.'

74. 'Good night, Mrs. Maloney. And thank *you*.'

75. And now, she told herself as she hurried back, all she was doing now, she was returning home to her husband and he was waiting for his supper; and she must cook it good, and make it as tasty as possible because the poor man was tired; and if when she entered the house, she happened to find anything unusual, or tragic, or terrible, then naturally it would be a shock and she would become frantic with grief and horror. Mind you she wasn't *expecting* to find anything. She was just going home with the vegetables on Thursday evening to cook supper for her husband.

76. That's the way, she told herself. Do everything right and natural. Keep things absolutely natural and there'll be no need for acting at all.

77. Therefore when she entered the kitchen by the back door, she was humming a little tune to herself and smiling.

78. 'Patrick!' she called. 'How are you darling?'

79. She put the parcel down on the table and went through into the living room; and when she saw him lying there on the floor with his legs doubled up and one arm twisted back underneath his body, it really was rather a shock. All the old love and longing for him for him welled up inside her, and she ran over to him, knelt down beside him, and began to cry her heart out. It was easy. No acting necessary. A few minutes later she got up and went to the phone. She knew the number of the police station, and when the man at the other end of the phone answered, she cried to him, 'Quick! Come quick! Patrick's dead!'

80. 'Who's speaking?'

81. 'Mrs. Maloney. Mrs. Patrick Maloney.'

82. 'You mean Patrick Maloney's dead?'

83. 'I think so,' she sobbed. 'He's lying on the floor and I think he's dead.'

84. 'Be right over,' the man said.

85. The car came very quickly, and when she opened the front door, two policemen walked in. She knew them both – she knew nearly all the men at that precinct – and she fell right into Jack Noonan's arms, weeping hysterically. He put her gently into a chair, then went over to join the other one, who was called O'Malley, kneeling by the body.

86. 'Is he dead?' she cried.

87. 'I'm afraid he is. What happened?'

88. Briefly, she told her story about going out to the grocer and coming back to find him on the floor. While she was talking, crying and talking, Noonan discovered a small patch of congealed blood on the dead man's head. He showed it to O'Malley who got up at once and hurried to the phone.

89. Soon other men began to come into the house. First a doctor, then two detectives, one of whom she knew by name. Later a police photographer arrived and took pictures, and a man who knew about fingerprints. There was a great deal of whispering and muttering beside the corpse, and the detectives kept asking her a lot of questions. But they always treated her kindly. She told her story again, this time from the beginning, when Patrick had come in, and she was sewing, and he was tired, so tired he hadn't wanted to go out for supper. She told how she had put the meat in the oven – 'It's there now, cooking' – and how she'd slipped out to the grocer for vegetables, and come back to find him lying on the floor.

90. 'Which grocer?' one of the detectives asked.

91. She told him, and he turned and whispered something to the other detective who immediately went out into the street.

92. In fifteen minutes he was back with a page of notes and there was more whispering, and through her sobbing she heard a few of the whispered phrases – '... acted quite normal ... very cheerful ... wanted to give him a good supper ... peas ... cheesecake ... impossible that she ...'.

93. After a while, the photographer and the doctor departed and two other men came in and took the corpse away on a stretcher. Then the fingerprint man went away. The two detectives remained, and so did the two policemen. They were exceptionally nice to her, and Jack Noonan asked if she wouldn't rather go somewhere else, to her sister's house perhaps, or to his own wife who would take care of her and put her up for the night.

94. No, she said, she didn't feel she could move even a yard at the moment. Would they mind awfully if she stayed just where she was until she felt better? She didn't feel too good at the moment, she really didn't.

95. Then hadn't she better lie down on the bed? Jack Noonan asked.

96. No she said, she'd like to stay right where she was, in this chair. A little later perhaps, when she felt better, she would move.

97. So they left her there while they went about their business searching the house. Occasionally one of the detectives asked her another question. Sometimes Jack Noonan spoke to her gently as he passed by. Her husband, he told her, had been killed by a blow on the back of the head administered with a heavy blunt instrument, almost certainly a large piece of metal. They were looking for the weapon. The murderer may have taken it with him, but on the other hand he may've thrown it away or hidden it somewhere on the premises.

98. 'It's the old story,' he said. 'Get the weapon, and you've got the man.'

99. Later one of the detectives came up and sat beside her. Did she know, he asked, of anything in the house that could've been used as the weapon? Would she mind having a look around to see if anything was missing – a very big spanner, for example or a heavy metal vase?

100. They didn't have any heavy metal vases, she said.

101. 'Or a big spanner?'

102. She didn't think they had a big spanner. But there might be some things like that in the garage.

103. The search went on. She knew that there were other policemen in the garden all around the house. She could hear their footsteps on the gravel outside, and sometimes she saw the flash of the torch through a chink in the curtains. It began to get late, nearly nine she noticed by the clock on the mantel. The four men searching the rooms seemed to be growing weary, a trifle exasperated.

104. 'Jack,' she said, the next time Sergeant Noonan went by, 'would you mind giving me a drink?'

105. 'Sure I'll give you a drink. You mean this whiskey?'

106. 'Yes, please. But just a small one. It might make me feel better.'

107. He handed her the glass.

108. 'Why don't you have one yourself,' she said. 'You must be awfully tired. Please do. You've been very good to me.'

109. 'Well,' he answered. 'It's not strictly allowed, but I might take just a drop to keep me going.'

110. One by one the others came in and they were persuaded to take a little nip of whiskey. They stood around rather awkwardly with the drinks in their hands, uncomfortable in her presence, trying to say consoling things to her. Sergeant Noonan wandered into the kitchen, came out quickly and said, 'Look, Mrs. Maloney, you know that oven of yours is still on, and the meat still inside?'

111. 'Oh *dear* me!' she cried. 'So it is!'

112. 'I better turn it off for you, hadn't I?'

113. 'Will you do that Jack? Thank you so much.'

114. When the sergeant returned the second time, she looked at him with her large, dark, tearful eyes. 'Jack Noonan,' she said.

115. 'Yes?'

116. 'Would you do me a small favour – you and these others?'

117. 'We can try, Mrs. Maloney.'

118. 'Well,' she said. 'Here you are and good friends of dear Patrick's too, and helping catch the man who killed him. You must be terribly hungry by now because it's long past your supper time, and I know Patrick would never forgive me, God bless his soul, if I allowed you to remain in this house without offering you decent hospitality. Why don't you eat up that lamb that's in the oven? It'll be cooked right by now.'

119. 'Wouldn't dream of it,' Sergeant Noonan said.

120. 'Please,' she begged. 'Please eat it. Personally I couldn't touch a thing, certainly not what's been in the house when he was here. But it's all right for you. It'll be a favour to me if you eat it up. Then you can go on with your work afterwards.'

121. There was a great deal of hesitating among the four policemen, but they were clearly hungry, and in the end they were persuaded to go into the kitchen and help themselves. The woman stayed where she was, listening to them through the open door, and she could hear them speaking among themselves, their voices thick and sloppy because their mouths were full of meat.

122. 'Have some more Charlie?'

123. 'No, better not finish it.'

124. 'She *wants* us to finish it. She said so. Be doing her a favour.'

125. 'Okay then. Give me some more.'

126. 'That's the hell of a big club that guy must have used to hit poor Patrick,' one of them was saying. 'The doc says his skull was smashed all to pieces just like from a sledge-hammer.'

127. 'That's why it ought to be easy to find.'
128. 'Exactly what I say.'
129. 'Whoever done it, they're not going to be carrying a thing like that around with them longer than they need.'
130. One of them belched.
131. 'Personally, I think it's right here on the premises.'
132. 'Probably right under our very noses. What do you think Jack?'
133. And in the other room, Mary Maloney began to giggle.

Roald Dahl

 THINKING THROUGH

First, share your answers to the **'First Thoughts'** questions you were given at the start of the story. Then work out the answer to the following question:

■ What happens to the murder weapon in this story?

NOW TRY THIS

There's a question below for you to discuss. Start by talking about it with a partner or in a group. You should be able in the end to come up with quite a few answers or parts to your answer.

- Are there any flaws in Mary's plan? Can you think of any way in which she might still get caught?

Share you answers with those from the rest of the class. When you get to this stage someone else in the class might be able to prove that one of your suggestions is wrong or doesn't work. You should end up with an agreed list of all the good answers to this question.

 LET'S GET TO WORK

If you've worked through Chapter 3 on *Snakes and Ladders*, you will have seen how Dilys Rose, who wrote that story, makes the reader feel sympathy for Lily. Lily's life is so awful that we can easily feel sorry for her. What makes *Lamb to the Slaughter* such an interesting and clever story is that we end up feeling sympathy for Mary too. Even though she is a murderer, Roald Dahl manipulates us until we want her to get away with her crime. In our study of the story we will see how Dahl does this.

The Maloney marriage

Mary obviously feels that their marriage is wonderful and perfect, and she seems to be trying very hard to make their life together a good one. One reason why we take her side in the story is that Patrick ruins all of this. When he tells Mary that he is leaving her this is a total shock for her.

At the start of the story, when Mary is alone in the house, Dahl builds up a picture of their happy life together.

NOW TRY THIS

Read paragraphs 1 to 9 again. Build up a table like the one below with details from the story to show how their life together is made to seem perfect. You can use quotations or references to do this. The first couple of examples have been done for you.

Paragraph	Detail	How their life seems perfect
1	*'The room was warm and clean'*	It makes Mary sound like a good housewife.
1	There is a lamp alight by the empty armchair	She is preparing for her husband coming home. Everything is the way he likes it.

Now you carry on from there. When you have finished, compare your answers with those of the rest of the class to make sure you have a full list.

So far so good. At this stage in the story everything about their marriage seems wonderful.

Patrick is obviously a very reliable man who always behaves in the same way and follows the same habits and routines. One example of this is that he always comes home at the same time, but Mary also knows exactly how he will behave and what he likes to do once he is home. Therefore the first signs that something is wrong are when Patrick begins to behave in ways that are slightly unusual or unexpected.

NOW TRY THIS

Read paragraphs 10 to 29 again. This time make a list of all the little details that suggest that something is wrong. The first couple have been done for you.

Paragraph	Detail
10	He drinks half his whiskey in one big swallow.
10	He goes to get another drink almost immediately.

Now you carry on from there.

Sympathy

So, even before Patrick tells Mary that he is leaving her, Dahl makes it seem as if Patrick is somehow spoiling the perfect atmosphere and happy home Mary has created. This is just part of how Roald Dahl manipulates the readers, making us feel sympathy for Mary and taking sides with her even while she is committing and covering up a horrible crime.

Another way our sympathy is directed towards Mary and away from Patrick is that **Patrick never gets to say much**. Because we don't really 'hear' from him, he never gets the chance to win our sympathy, even though he is the victim of a horrid murder, killed from behind in his own home with no chance to defend himself.

When Patrick does get to speak, **his words make us dislike him**. At first he speaks very abruptly. His short sentences like, '*Sit down*,' and, '*I don't want it*,' make him sound as if he is being rude to his wife when she is only trying to please him.

The one time in the story when he does speak in longer sentences is when he is telling her that he's going to leave her. We never find out what he actually says about why he is leaving. Perhaps if we knew his reasons we would be a little more understanding, so the writer deliberately does not allow us to hear why Patrick is ending the marriage. We do get to hear what Patrick says just before and just after the actual bad news that he breaks to Mary.

NOW TRY THIS

Look at the following things Patrick says in paragraphs 36 and 38. Each one actually makes him seem even worse. Can you explain why? Complete the table. The first one has been done for you as an example.

What he says	Why this makes him seem even worse
'*I've decided the only thing to do is to tell you right away.*'	She's heavily pregnant but he sees nothing wrong with his timing in telling her now.
'*I hope you won't blame me too much.*'	
'*there really needn't be any fuss … It wouldn't be good for my job.*'	

NOW TRY THIS

Patrick speaks just one more time in the story. His last words could be viewed as just another way of rejecting Mary, and rejecting everything she has done for him. He tells her in paragraph 44: '*For God's sake ... Don't make supper for me. I'm going out.*' Before we let him die, try to answer the following question. There is no right or wrong answer – it's more important that you can back up your answer with evidence from the story.

■ Do you feel any sympathy for Patrick at all? If you do, why do you feel this way?

The whole story is told to us from Mary's **point of view**. For example:

■ She is there on her own at the start of the story and we get to know her first as a good wife and someone who seems as if she is looking forward to being a good mother.

■ Although other characters come and go we are always 'with' Mary.

■ We only know what is happening because she sees or hears all the action, or because she takes part in it.

■ We know what people say because they say these things to Mary or because, as with the detectives at the end, she overhears them.

■ There are times, for example in paragraph 8, when we even seem to be listening in on her thoughts and feelings.

The fact that Roald Dahl sticks so closely to her point of view throughout the story is one major technique he uses to make us sympathise with her.

NOW TRY THIS

There are other reasons too why we feel sympathy for Mary. Answer the following questions:

1. How can we almost justify her killing Patrick, or at least understand why she feels the need to do it?
2. Read paragraph 39 again. What evidence is there that Mary may be in shock and not thinking clearly?
3. Read paragraph 41 again. What other evidence is there in this paragraph that Mary may be in shock and not thinking clearly?
4. Read paragraph 50 again. Explain how her thoughts in that paragraph mean that we are more likely to want her to get away with her crime.
5. Read paragraph 79 again. Explain how what she does in that paragraph makes us feel sympathetic towards her.

NOW TRY THIS

We've now looked very carefully at how Dahl builds up our sympathy for Mary throughout the story. There's just one more thing you need to think about here. There is no right or wrong answer – it's very much about your personal response to her as a character. Answer the following question:

■ At the end of the story, when Mary starts to laugh, do you still feel so sympathetic towards her? In a couple of sentences explain why you feel the way you do.

The cover-up

We've already looked the reason why Mary decides that she must not get caught. We are told in paragraph 51:

'she certainly wasn't prepared to take a chance.'

This story seems to be set in the USA, where many states used to have, and some still have, the death penalty for murder. (If you have time, you might want to look for the other clues in the story that hint to us that it is set in the USA, and not in Britain, even though Roald Dahl was a British writer.) From then on the whole story is about how she covers up the murder.

Twice **she rehearses for situations** she is about to get in to.

NOW TRY THIS

Read paragraphs 52 to 60.

1. What is the first situation she practises for?
2. How exactly does she practise for this?
3. Think about what happens later on in the story, once the police have arrived. How do we know that her little performance in the shop has been successful?

Her first rehearsal is mainly about trying out the words she's planning to use. Eventually those words, her voice, and her facial expression are convincing. Her second rehearsal goes a bit deeper. This time she prepares a set of feelings, and she even convinces herself.

Read paragraphs 75 to 77.

4. What is the second situation she practises for?
5. What does she tell herself about this situation?
6. How do we know that she manages to convince herself?

Her **trip to Sam's shop** is very clever. First of all it gives her an alibi. Sam will be able to remember talking to her at the time when the murder was supposedly happening in her house.

There is more to it than that though. Almost everything she says is designed to make her seem not just innocent but perfect. She gives the impression that she is a fantastic wife and that everything is as wonderful as usual.

NOW TRY THIS

Copy the following table into your notebook and complete it. The first entry has been done for you as an example.

What Mary says/does	How this covers up the crime
She smiles brightly at Sam.	She looks too happy to have been through any kind of unusual experience.
She says Patrick is tired and doesn't want to go out.	
She mentions that they usually go out on Thursdays.	
She tells Sam she has taken some lamb out of the freezer.	
She seems worried about the risk of cooking the lamb from frozen.	
She asks Sam to suggest a pudding.	
She tells Sam that Patrick loves cheesecake.	

The final stage of the cover-up is Mary's triumph in getting the police to eat the leg of lamb and so destroy the murder weapon. Once they do this all the forensic evidence, such as fingerprints, any traces of Patrick's blood or any of his hair that might have got stuck to the frosty surface of the lamb is gone. There's no weapon to link the crime to Mary.

Mary softens them up first of all by getting them to have some whiskey. We'll look at this in more detail when we go on to study the detectives. It's worth noticing though that once people have had an alcoholic drink their resistance is likely to be lowered and they can be talked into things more easily. Also, once she has got them to do something 'bad' by persuading them to have a drink when they should not be drinking on duty, it is actually more likely that they will do something 'good' to make up for this and eat the meat out of kindness to her.

Read paragraphs 116 to 120. Pick out the six reasons Mary uses to persuade the investigating officers to eat the meat.

It's not clear in the story whether Mary always plans to get the police to eat the meat, or whether the idea only comes to her after Sergeant Noonan reminds her that the lamb is still in the oven. Perhaps she always plans to get them to eat it, and she deliberately leads them towards this idea by getting them to accept a drink first. If you agree with this idea then in paragraph 111 when she is told that the lamb is still there and says 'Oh *dear* me!' she is only acting at being surprised. On the other hand perhaps the shocking and unusual things that have happened tonight have made her forget about the meat and she really is surprised to be reminded that it is still there.

Discuss the following question with a partner, a group, or the class:

■ Do you think Mary always planned to make the police eat the meat, or did she just think of it when they reminded her that the lamb was still in the oven?

Back up your answer with evidence from the story.

Whether or not she plans this last part of the cover-up, it certainly works. We can't help admiring how cleverly Mary gets away with her crime. Remember that everything else we know about her suggests she has probably led a quiet life and been a good, or even boring, person. Suddenly she becomes cunning and intelligent, and is always one step ahead of everyone, even experienced police officers.

The detectives

Another reason why we want Mary to get away with her crime is that we end up disliking the detectives. Because we don't like them, we don't want them to catch her out.

One reason why we dislike the policemen is because they seem rather **stupid**, and not very good at their job. Most murder victims are killed by someone they know very well. An adult who is murdered is more likely to have been killed by his or her own partner than by any other person. In other words, Mary should immediately be the number one suspect. As well as being Patrick's wife she also admits she was the last person to see him alive.

At first the police do seem to be checking up on Mary.

NOW TRY THIS

Read paragraphs 89 to 92 and answer the following questions:

1. What story does Mary tell the police?
2. What do they do to investigate this story?
3. Can you think of anything else they could have done which would test more thoroughly whether or not she is telling the truth?

However, once the detective comes back from the shop, they seem to abandon any idea that Mary might be responsible. Look at this extract from paragraphs 97 and 98.

> So they left her there while they went about their business searching the house. Occasionally one of the detectives asked her another question. Sometimes Jack Noonan spoke to her gently as he passed by. Her husband, he told her, had been killed by a blow on the back of the head administered with a heavy blunt instrument, almost certainly a large piece of metal. They were looking for the weapon. The murderer may have taken it with him, but on the other hand he may've thrown it away or hidden it somewhere on the premises.
>
> 'It's the old story,' he said. 'Get the weapon, and you've got the man.'

Now answer these questions:

4. Which three little words in the extract tell us that the detectives are looking for someone very different from Mary? Quote them.
5. How do those words tell us this?

As stated earlier, most victims are murdered by their partners. You might also find it useful to know that in these cases most of the victims tend to be female, and the murderers are usually male. This may be one reason why the police don't press their investigation of Mary. Another reason may be because of the way in which the murder is carried out. They can tell that Patrick has been killed

> 'by a blow on the back of the head administered with a heavy blunt instrument, almost certainly a large piece of metal.'

Perhaps they just think this is a more male way to kill someone. They certainly seem to think that only a man would use a weapon in this way. They don't realise that Mary gained strength from her anger.

Another reason why we dislike the police is because they seem rather **greedy**, and seem to put their own appetites before the case they are investigating. This is most obvious at the end of the story when they all stop work at once to eat the leg of lamb. However, they have already indulged in a way they are not supposed to.

Think about any TV programmes or films you have seen in which police come to investigate a crime. There is a cliché that often comes up in these films and programmes: a member of the public will offer the police a drink and the officer says something like, 'Not while I'm on duty.'

The police in this story are not so professional.

NOW TRY THIS

Read paragraphs 108 to 110 again and answer the following questions:

1. Which words prove that Jack Noonan knows he should not accept the whiskey Mary offers him? Quote them.
2. Which words show us that **all** the police end up accepting a drink and breaking orders? Quote them.

As well as being rather stupid and greedy, the police also seem rather **uncouth** and **bad-mannered**. When Mary listens to them from outside the kitchen door their voices are '*thick and sloppy because their mouths were full of meat.*' Your parents probably brought you up not to talk with your mouth full, but the detectives' manners don't seem very good.

NOW TRY THIS

Look at the last few paragraphs of the story. Which other sentence also points out the bad manners of the police? Quote it.

The police in this story come across as stupid, greedy and ill-mannered. Mary is a complete **contrast** to them.

NOW TRY THIS

Copy the table below into your notebook to show the contrast between Mary and the police. Some of the details have been filled in already but you will have to work out the rest. You may want to work with a partner to do this.

The police	Mary
stupid	intelligent
1 They give up investigating Mary very quickly.	1
2	2
greedy	not greedy
1 They accept whiskey.	1
2	
ill-mannered	polite
1	1
2	2

The last thing Dahl does to turn us against the police is to make sure that, at the end of the story, the joke is on them. The technique he uses here is called **irony**. Irony is quite a complex idea to understand, but it often involves a situation where there is a lot more going on than some people realise. This may lead to people saying things without appreciating the full meaning and importance of what they say.

The last two things said by the police in this story are very **ironic**. One of them says that the murder weapon is probably '*right here on the premises*'. A second agrees and says that it is, '*probably right under our very noses*'. As they say this they are actually eating the weapon, and it's under their noses because it is on its way into their mouths. The final irony is that the policemen who are supposed to be solving the crime are actually destroying the weapon. When Mary laughs at them, we feel like laughing at them too because they don't know how easily they've been fooled.

Possible essay tasks

Now that you've finished studying this story, you could tackle the following essay questions. Remember to follow the advice from Chapter 9 on how to write literature essays.

Above the prose essay choices on the exam paper you'll see the following words:

> **Answers to questions in this section should refer to such relevant features as: content, character, theme, imagery...**

Now look at the essay choices:

- Choose a short story in which one of the main characters has to make a decision.

  Explain what the decision is and show how it is important for the rest of the story.

or

- Choose a novel or a short story which has an important turning point that changes things for one of the characters.

  Show how the story builds up to the turning point and say how it is important for the character.

6 Poetry: Child On Top Of A Greenhouse

 GETTING IN

We're going to study a poem. Before you read it, think about the following questions. You should share your answers with a partner, a small group, or your class.

- Can you think of a time when you were a child and did something you knew you were not supposed to do? How did you feel about it?

- Can you think of a time when you were a child and did something you knew was dangerous? How did you feel about it?

 FIRST THOUGHTS

Theodore Roethke (you pronounce this *Thee-oh-door Rooth-kih*) was an American writer, though his family originally came from Germany. His father Otto and his uncle Charles owned a greenhouse business. He wrote this poem when he was an adult but in it he is remembering something he did when he was a child. As you read the poem think about the following questions.

- Where is the child?

- Is he supposed to be there? How can you tell?

Child on Top of a Greenhouse

The wind billowing out the seat of my britches,
My feet crackling splinters of glass and dried putty,
The half grown chrysanthemums staring up like accusers,
Up through the streaked glass, flashing with sunlight,
A few white clouds all rushing eastward,
A line of elms plunging and tossing like horses,
And everyone, everyone pointing up and shouting!

Theodore Roethke

 THINKING THROUGH

First share your answers to the **'First Thoughts'** questions you were given at the start of the poem. Then work out the answer to this question:

■ This poem is only seven lines long. It describes six different things the young Roethke noticed while he was on top of the greenhouse. One of those details needs two whole lines to describe it, while the other five mini-memories just need one line each. Which two lines together describe one single detail? Quote them.

NOW TRY THIS

Now that you have worked out what the six different details are that Roethke remembers in the poem, can you draw a picture for each one? You could do this as a cartoon strip in six pictures, with the right line(s) of the poem written under the boxes like captions. Or you could work in a group and produce one larger picture for each memory. If you do this you should write the right line(s) of the poem at the bottom of your picture. These could be displayed in your classroom.

 ## LET'S GET TO WORK

This looks like a very short and simple poem. You could probably learn it by heart very easily. (This might be a good idea. Then you'll be able to quote from it in any essays you write.) However, poets make the language work very hard. Even a short poem can be full of cleverly used techniques. We're going to look at how Roethke uses **senses**, **tenses**, **similes**, **punctuation** and **repetition** to hint at the boy's feelings and even to suggest what life in the Roethke family might have been like.

Senses

   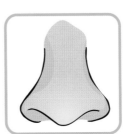 

NOW TRY THIS

Make a list of your five senses.

NOW TRY THIS

This poem is full of details which the boy senses. You have already divided the poem up into the six different mini-memories or details in it. One at a time, write the line(s) for each mini-memory in your notebook. At the end of each mini-memory, in capital letters, write the sense he is using there. Then answer these questions:

1. Are any of his five senses not used at all in the poem?
2. Do any of the mini-memories seem to come from more than one sense?
3. Which sense(s) does he seem to use most in the poem?

As we look at each technique Roethke uses in this poem, we are always going to ask ourselves the same question:

- What effect does Roethke achieve by using this technique?

'What effect does Roethke achieve …?' is just a another way of saying, 'Why does he choose to write this way?' or, 'What is he trying to do to me as I read this?' So, answer this question now:

- What effect does Roethke achieve with the poem by using all this detail from the boy's **senses**?

Tense

In the English language, **tenses** help us to talk or write about **when** something happens:

- The **past** tense helps us to talk about things that have **already happened**.
  e.g. I **went** to Spain on holiday last year.

- The **present** tense helps us to talk about what is **happening now**.
  e.g. My auntie **lives** in Spain. She **has** a villa on the Costa del Sol.

- The **future tense** helps us to talk about what **will happen**, or what **is going to happen**.
  e.g. I **am going to stay** with my auntie next year. I **will be** in Spain all summer but I **will need to get** a job out there.

You can work out the tense of something by looking at the **verbs**, the **doing words**.

NOW TRY THIS

Read through the poem again. As you read it, make a list of all the verbs in the poem. Then answer these questions:

1. Which tense does the poem seem to be written in?
2. Can you explain why this is an odd tense to choose for this poem?
3. Which tense would you expect this poem to be written in?

NOW TRY THIS

Can you rewrite the poem, changing or adding as few words as you need to, to put it in the tense that you would expect a poem like this to be written in?

That brings us back to that important question we have to answer about every technique. Try to answer it now:

■ What effect does Roethke achieve with the poem by using the **present tense** instead of the past tense?

Similes

A simile is a comparison of two things, made by using the word *like* or the word *as*. For example:

He swims as smoothly as a dolphin.

or

She has a nose like half a strawberry.

Similes help us to picture something when we read about it or hear about it. Perhaps we have never been to a particular place, or seen a particular person or object. In that case a simile can help us to imagine it or him or her by comparing the unknown thing or person to something or someone that we do know about.

NOW TRY THIS

There are two similes in the poem. First of all find them and write them down.

Then answer these questions:

1. What does the first simile tell you about the way the boy feels?
2. What does the second simile tell you about the weather?

Both of these similes are visual images – things the boy saw. You'll have noticed them already when you were looking for details from the boy's five senses.

Now go back to the important question we have to answer about every technique. Try to answer it now:

■ What effect does Roethke achieve with the poem by using **similes** for these visual details from his memory?

Punctuation

Punctuation means all the other little marks that go on a page of writing, apart from the actual words themselves.

NOW TRY THIS

Do you recognise the names of these punctuation marks? Write them down in a list in your notebook. Beside each one, draw the mark itself. Make sure you get each mark to sit on the right part of the line.

	full stop		comma
	question mark		speech marks
	exclamation mark		dash
	bracket		apostrophe
	colon		

NOW TRY THIS

Read through the poem again. Each time you meet a punctuation mark for the first time, write its name. Then answer these questions:

1. Which punctuation marks are used in this poem?
2. How many times is each of these marks used?
3. How many sentences are there in this poem?

What you should be noticing is that Roethke uses a comma at the end of each line, except at the end of the last one, when he uses an exclamation mark instead. You should also have noticed that the poem is just one long sentence.

These commas are used to divide the one sentence of the poem into many **clauses**. A **clause** is a chunk of a sentence. Some clauses do not make sense on their own, but need to be with other clauses to make up a complete and grammatical sentence.

In fact, if you look at it really carefully, you might notice that this whole poem is still not actually one whole and grammatically correct sentence. It doesn't really have a main verb in it. If we wanted to make the poem have perfect grammar, we'd need to add a few words at the start. You could make it begin with something like, 'I can remember,' or, 'From the greenhouse roof I noticed,' and then everything else would follow on from there. Roethke is far more interested in telling us about his memories in a way that affects us than he is in using perfect grammar. He knows how to write grammatically, but it isn't the most important thing here.

That leads us back to that 'effect' question again. It's in two parts this time. Answer it now:

■ What effect does Roethke achieve with the poem by punctuating it so that it is just **one sentence with many clauses**?

■ What effect does Roethke achieve by using the closing **exclamation mark**?

Repetition

Repetition means using a word or a phrase more than once. Of course there are some words that we have to use a lot, especially some of the little words in our language like *a* and *the* and *is* and so on. When we talk about a writer using repetition we mean that he or she **deliberately** repeats a word or a phrase so that it is used **more often than you would expect**. When we find an example of this kind of repetition, it begins to let us know what is important to the writer, or to the speaker.

NOW TRY THIS

Read through the poem again. You should be able to find one fairly noticeable example of repetition. Can you quote the line in which it is used?

Here we are back at that 'effect' question again. Answer it now:

■ What effect does Roethke achieve with the poem by using this particular example of **repetition**?

Now that we have looked at how Roethke uses these five techniques, we will see how he manages to suggest a great deal about different people's feelings, and how he even gives us some hints about life in the boy's family.

The centre of attention

We have already looked very closely at the way Roethke organises the details and memories in the poem. The last line is about people watching him from below. First, let's think about those people. We are told that all of them are '*pointing up and shouting!*' They are all united against him. Nobody is on his side. They clearly feel they are right.

NOW TRY THIS

Answer the following questions:

1. Who do you think those people are?
2. How do you think they feel? Why would they feel that way?
3. What do you think they might be shouting up at him?

There is a fairly strong hint earlier in the poem that the boy does know he's not meant to be up there, and that he is aware he's done something wrong.

4. Can you quote the line that suggests this?

Those people might be quite annoyed (or even very annoyed) if they realised that their shouting was not having the effect that they wanted it to have.

5. How does the boy feel about being watched? Support your answer with evidence from the poem.

Neglect

Not everything that poets choose to write about is true to their life. Even if they take stories from their own lives to write about, that doesn't mean everything in the poem is strictly true. However, it might be useful for you at this stage to know that the Roethke family wasn't an exactly happy one.

His father drank. (We'll find out more about this in the next chapter when we look at another poem Roethke wrote.) His father and his uncle Charles fell out when Charles let the greenhouse business get into money trouble. Charles eventually committed suicide and Roethke's father Otto died of cancer just two months later, when Roethke was only 15.

Perhaps the business was already heading for trouble when the young Roethke climbed up on the roof that day. There are certainly signs that things are being neglected, not being taken care of.

NOW TRY THIS

Read the prompts and then answer the questions that follow.

A dirty greenhouse won't let much light through, which means that the plants inside will not grow as well as they ought to.

1. Which words in the poem tell us that the greenhouse is dirty?

A greenhouse that is broken will let in draughts. In the colder air, the plants will not grow as well as they ought to.

2. Which words in the poem tell us that the grass is broken?

There are also hints in the poem that the boy himself is not being cared for as well as he should be.

3. Which words in the poem tell us that his clothes are torn?

It's fair to remind you again that we should not think that everything in a writer's work is telling you something about that writer's life. It's already been suggested that the broken, dirty glass and the boy's torn clothes suggest neglect. But there is another interpretation too.

4. Can you think of any other reason why the glass might be broken and the boy's clothes might be torn?

Danger

It's not very safe for the boy to be up there, which might be why everyone is shouting and trying to get him down.

One thing you ought to have noticed is that the weather is rather wild, and that there is a chance he might simply get blown off the top of the roof.

■   Which line of the poem tells us that the wind is wild?

NOW TRY THIS

Why else is it dangerous for him to be up there? How many other reasons can you think of?

Point of view

All of the techniques we have looked at, and all the details Roethke puts in the poem, make us see this memory from his point of view. Although it is a very short poem, just 57 words long, it makes his childhood memory seem real, complete and vivid.

In the next chapter we are going to look at another poem by Roethke, which describes another childhood memory. Again we will see things from his point of view, although this time we will be able to work out a little more about how the adults feel.

Possible essay tasks

Now that you've finished studying this poem, you could tackle the following essay questions. Remember to follow the advice from Chapter 9 on how to write literature essays.

Above the poetry essay choices on the exam paper you'll see the following words:

> Answers to questions in this section should refer to such relevant features as: word choice, theme, imagery...

Now look at the essay choices:

- Choose a poem about an incident or an event.

  Say what happens in the poem and show how the poet has used particular words and phrases to give you a clear description of what happened.

OR

- Choose a poem which creates a particular mood or atmosphere for you.

  Say what the mood or atmosphere is and go on to show how it is created by the language of the poem.

7

Poetry: My Papa's Waltz

GETTING IN

We're going to study another Roethke poem. Before you read it, think about the following question. You should share your answers with a partner, a small group, or your class.

■ Think back to when you were a child. Can you remember some game you enjoyed playing, or something you enjoyed doing, with an older member of your family?

FIRST THOUGHTS

As you read through this poem for the first time, try to answer the following questions:

1. How many people are involved in this poem? Who are they?

2. Where does this poem take place?

3. What is happening in this poem?

My Papa's Waltz

The whiskey on your breath
Could make a small boy dizzy;
But I hung on like death:
Such waltzing was not easy.

We romped until the pans
Slid from the kitchen shelf;
My mother's countenance
Could not unfrown itself.

The hand that held my wrist
Was battered on one knuckle;
At every step you missed
My right hand scraped a buckle.

You beat time on my head
With a palm caked hard by dirt,
Then waltzed me off to bed
Still clinging to your shirt.

Theodore Roethke

 THINKING THROUGH

First share your answers to the **'First Thoughts'** question you were given at the start of the poem.

The other Roethke poem in this book, *Child on Top of a Greenhouse*, seems to be describing something that only happened once. *My Papa's Waltz*, though, seems to describe something that happened quite often during Roethke's childhood.

NOW TRY THIS

Work out the answers to these questions:

1. Which words in the first verse help us to know that this kind of thing happened often?
2. How do those words tell us this?

LET'S GET TO WORK

This is another short and simple-looking poem. It uses rhyme and rhythm, which the previous Roethke poem we looked at did not. Once again we are going to look at how Roethke uses details from his senses. We'll see how he creates a mood in the poem and how he gives away a lot about the relationships within the family. Most especially, we will see how such a small poem actually tells us a lot about Roethke's father.

Senses

NOW TRY THIS

Like the previous Roethke poem, this one is full of details which the boy senses. Now read through the poem again. Beside each sense, write down the line(s) from the poem which show him remembering something that came to him through that particular sense. Set it out as shown in the table below. The first one has been done for you.

Sense	Detail
Smell	*'The whisky on your breath'*
Taste	
Touch	
Hearing	
Sight	

There is one more detail in the poem that might be a piece of sense information. The dizziness that the boy feels comes at least partly from his sense of sight. That's why if you have ever felt dizzy or car-sick you probably found that it helped a bit if you closed your eyes. Doing this shut down your sense of sight so that you did not have to look at things whirling past you.

Implication

Implication is the technique of suggesting things to the reader. A good writer will not always need to tell us everything outright. Instead he or she can **imply** or suggest things by using carefully chosen words and phrases. Let's see what you can work out without Roethke actually telling you:

1. How old, and how big, do you think the boy was when he waltzed with his father?

2. Now let's make sure you didn't come up with your answer just by looking at the picture. By quoting from the poem, show how you worked out the boy's age and size.

If you think about what is happening in the poem, it sounds at first as if it could be quite frightening. A man who seems to be drunk is dancing a rather small boy around the room. The boy seems to be clinging on desperately, as if he might be scared of falling off. The dance is rough enough to make things come flying off the shelves, and clumsy enough for the boy's hands to get scraped. Yet we know somehow that the boy is actually enjoying himself.

3. Which word in verse 2 tells us that the boy enjoyed this waltzing?

4. How does that word tell you this?

Roethke's mother's feelings are also implied to us. Although she does not speak, we can tell what she thinks of this waltzing round her kitchen.

5. How does she feel?

6. Which lines in the poem tell you this? Quote them.

7. Can you give at least two reasons why she might have felt this way? Back up each reason by using a quotation from the poem.

The father

In 1925, when he was 17 years old, and his father had been dead for two years, Roethke wrote this:

'A great story could be written about my father, for in many ways he was a truly great man. I have never found anyone remotely like him in life or in literature.'

That's an interesting thing to say. Roethke obviously admired his father and loved him. However, as soon as he says that his father was a great man '*in many ways*', we realise that there must also have been '*many ways*' in which his father was not a great man. Some of these are suggested in the poem.

NOW TRY THIS

You might want to do this with a partner, or in a group. Take a new page, or a new piece of paper. Set out a table like the one below. Try to think of as many good and bad things about the boy's father as you can. The first one has been done for you.

The boy's father

Good side	Bad side
He spends time playing with his son.	

NOW TRY THIS

Now that you have thought about his good side and his bad side, answer these questions about the poet's father:

1. What kind of personality do you think he had? Back up your answer with evidence from the poem.

We already know that Roethke's father owned a greenhouse and worked with plants. However, even if you didn't know that, you might be able to work it out from the poem.

2. Which two different parts of the poem suggest or imply the sort of work Otto Roethke did? Quote them.

We can also tell that Roethke's father is quite far under the influence of drink as he dances with his son. He's drunk enough to make him clumsy.

3. Which two different parts of the poem suggest or imply Otto Roethke's clumsiness? Quote them.

Rhythm and rhyme

Of all the poems in this book, *My Papa's Waltz* is the only one that deliberately uses strongly patterened rhythm and rhyme to gain a particular effect. To see how Roethke does this, and to work out what effect he is aiming for, we first need to examine the rhythm and rhyme.

Let's start with the **rhyme**. Take another look at the first verse:

> The whiskey on your breath
> Could make a small boy dizzy;
> But I hung on like death:
> Such waltzing was not easy.

NOW TRY THIS

Which words rhyme with each other? Copy and complete the following sentences in your notebook:

In verse 1 of 'My Papa's Waltz', the word _____ at the end of line 1 rhymes with the word _____ at the end of line ____. The word _____ at the end of line ___ rhymes with the word _____ at the end of line ____.

NOW TRY THIS

Now look at the other verses. You should be able to see a pattern emerging. Can you now complete the following sentence in your notebook?

In each verse of 'My Papa's Waltz', the first line rhymes with the _____ line, and the _____ line rhymes with the _____ line.

Now it's time to look at the **rhythm**. A line of poetry, or speech or writing, can have rhythm just as a line of music has rhythm. In music, the rhythm is made up of beats arranged into short groups called bars.

In speech and writing, the rhythm comes from the pattern of **syllables**. Syllables are the individual chunks of sound in a word. For example, here's the first line of the poem again, broken down into the individual syllables:

The/ whis/ key/ on/ your/ breath

The line has six syllables. Now take a look at the whole first verse, broken down into syllables:

The/ whis/ key/ on/ your/ breath
Could/ make/ a/ small/ boy/ di/ zzy;
But/ I/ hung/ on/ like/ death:
Such/ waltz/ ing/ was/ not/ ea/ sy.

NOW TRY THIS

Copy and complete the following sentences in your notebook to help you explain the rhythm of that verse:

> In verse 1 of 'My Papa's Waltz', the first line and the _____ line each have _____ syllables. The other two lines, line ____ and line _____ each have _____ syllables.

NOW TRY THIS

Now look at the other verses. You should be able to see a pattern emerging. Discuss this with your group or class. Come to an agreement and write one or two sentences in your jotter to describe the rhythm of this poem.

Roethke has done something else with the rhythm of this poem. The '*waltz*' mentioned in the title is a piece of music which follows the rule of having three beats to the bar. If you were to set this poem to music, it would be in waltz time – it could be sung in time to a tune that has three beats per bar. If you feel like putting your teacher on the spot, ask him or her to demonstrate this for you!

This brings us back to the question of effect. We have already looked at how the word '*romped*' in the poem tells us that the boy enjoyed the dance, even though it might seem at first as if it was all rather rough and could have been quite scary. Using such strong rhyme and rhythm is another way for Roethke to signal to us that the poem is about a happy memory. They give the poem a light, non-serious feel, so we can again feel that the boy was not afraid of blundering around with his drunken father.

Family relationships

We noted earlier that this poem hints at quite a of detail about the relationships within Roethke's family. There are three people involved here, and each of them has some of kind of relationship with the other two. It's a bit like a triangle:

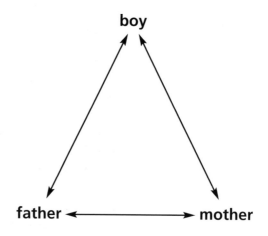

NOW TRY THIS

You might want to work with a partner or a group to do this. Answer the following questions:

1. How do you think the boy feels towards his father? Back up your answer with evidence from the poem.
2. How do you think the boy feels towards his mother? Back up your answer with evidence from the poem.
3. How do you think the father feels towards his son? Back up your answer with evidence from the poem.
4. How do you think the father feels towards his wife? Back up your answer with evidence from the poem.
5. How do you think the mother feels towards her son? Back up your answer with evidence from the poem.
6. How do you think the mother feels towards her husband? Back up your answer with evidence from the poem.

Word choice

Of course every word a writer uses is chosen in some sense. However, writers make particular choices to use certain kinds of words that help them put across their message or tell their story. We've already looked at the carefully-chosen word 'romped' and what it suggests to us.

There are two places in the poem where Roethke uses a word or a phrase to suggest there is an element of speed, and even danger, here.

- One of them is in verse 1. Can you find it?

- One of them is in verse 4. Can you find it?

He also uses a word that is interesting because it is so serious and formal. In verse 2 he writes about, '*My mother's countenance*'. *Countenance* is a rather showy word but it just means 'face', so why doesn't he just write 'face'? One reason is that if he did, it wouldn't rhyme with '*pans*' in the first line of the verse, and at least using '*countenance*' creates a partial rhyme. The second reason is even more clever. By using a very serious word **for** his mother's face, he reminds us that she has a very serious expression **on** her face.

Possible essay tasks

Now that you've finished studying this poem, you could tackle the following essay questions. Remember to follow the advice from Chapter 9 on how to write literature essays.

Above the poetry essay choices on the exam paper you'll see the following words:

> Answers to questions in this section should refer to such relevant features as: word choice, theme, imagery...

Now look at the essay choices:

■ Choose a poem which focuses on a person's experience.

Say what the experience is and how the particular words and phrases the poet uses help you to understand how the person feels.

or

■ Choose a poem which describes the feelings of a character.

Say what the feelings are and then go on to show how some of the words and phrases make the feelings clear to you.

8

Poetry: The Identification

 GETTING IN

So far in this book we have studied two poems told to us from a child's point of view, although a grown man wrote them. Those poems were also about childhood memories and things that had happened in the past.

This poem is different. It comes from an adult's point of view. It is also told in the present tense. The writer, Roger McGough, wanted his readers to feel as if they were reading about the events in the poem at the moment they were happening, not later on.

It might help you to know that McGough was inspired to write the poem after he saw a father being interviewed on the TV news. A terrorist bomb had killed the man's teenage son. The boy had no link to the terrorists; he was just unlucky enough to be in the wrong place at the wrong time.

Before you read the poem, think about the following question. You should share your answers with a partner, a small group, or your class.

■ Is there something you do that your parents don't know about, something they wouldn't want you to do?

 FIRST THOUGHTS

As you read through this poem for the first time, try to answer the following questions:

1. Where do you think the poem is set?
2. Who is speaking in the poem?
3. Who do you think he is speaking **to**?
4. Who is he speaking **about**?
5. Why has the speaker come to this place?

The Identification

So you think it's Stephen?
Then I'd best make sure.
Be on the safe side as it were.
Ah, there's been a mistake. The hair
5   you see, it's black, now Stephen's fair…
What's that? The explosion?
Of course, burnt black. Silly of me.
I should have known. Then let's get on.

The face. Is that a face I ask?
10 That mask of charred wood,
blistered, scarred – could
that have been a child's face?
The sweater, where intact, looks
in fact all too familiar.
15 But one must be sure.

The scoutbelt. Yes that's his.
I recognise the studs he hammered in
not a week ago. At the age
when boys get clothes-conscious
20 now you know. Remove all trace of doubt.
Pull out every splinter of hope.

Pockets. Empty the pockets.
Handkerchief? Could be any schoolboy's.
Dirty enough. Cigarettes?
25 Oh this can't be Stephen.
I don't allow him to smoke you see.
He wouldn't disobey me, not his father.

But that's his penknife. That's his all right.
And that's his key on the key ring
30 Gran gave him just the other night.
So this must be him.

I think I know what happened…
about the cigarettes.
No doubt he was minding them
35 for one of the older boys.
Yes that's it.
That's him.
That's our Stephen.

Roger McGough

 # THINKING THROUGH

First share your answers to the **'First Thoughts'** questions you were given at the start of the poem.

 # LET'S GET TO WORK

You would expect this poem to be expressed in quite simple, un-poetic language. One reason for this is because it is just supposed to be an ordinary man talking. Also, when you think about the horrible situation he is in, you would not expect him to be putting his thoughts into any kind of fancy language. However, as we study this poem we will see that McGough has done some very clever things with the language, although he has hidden them inside something that seems like everyday speech.

NOW TRY THIS

Answer the following questions. They are fairly basic ones, which will help you to make some initial notes about the poem.

1. What has happened to Stephen? **Quote** the line that first tells you this for sure.
2. What is the connection between Stephen and the speaker? **Quote** the line that tells you this.
3. There is only one voice, half a conversation here. Who do you think the other person in the room is, the one we don't hear from?
4. What emotion do you think the speaker is feeling when he says, '*Ah, there's been a mistake*'? Why do you think he feels this way?
5. What do you think he is feeling when he says '*Silly of me. I should have known. Then let's get on.*'?

NOW TRY THIS

Starting with the sweater, list all the evidence that this is Stephen. Then, beside each piece of evidence, write down whether it is very convincing, quite convincing or not at all convincing. Set it out as shown below. The first one has been done for you.

Item	Convincing?	Reason
sweater	quite	The father does say it looks '*too familiar*' but perhaps the dead boy just went to the same shop as Stephen.

NOW TRY THIS

Answer the next set of questions. They are all about things the father says as he considers the evidence the other adult shows him.

1. Look at the first line of the poem. What must the speaker have been told already?
2. Look at line 6, '*What's that? The explosion?*'. Write down the exact words you think the other person in the room must have just said.
3. Look at verse 2. What is the first thing that shocks him?
4. Which phrase in line 14 tells us the speaker is giving up hope?
5. Look at line 18. Why does his father particularly comment that Stephen hammered studs into his belt, '*not a week ago.*'?
6. '*At the age when boys get clothes-conscious*' (line 19) What does this mean? How old do you think Stephen is?
7. Look at line 21. What do you think the expression '*splinter of hope*' means?
8. How is he able to dismiss the evidence of the handkerchief in line 23?
9. '*Oh, this can't be Stephen.*' (line 25) What leads the speaker to this conclusion? Do you agree with how he decides this?

Theme

As we have discovered already, the **theme** of a poem (or of any other kind of text) is the big idea behind it. The theme is something the writer wants you to think about or learn about. It may be an idea the writer is trying to explore. A theme should be something that you can express using just one or two simple words. If you want a fuller explanation of what we mean when we talk about theme, look again at the end of Chapter 3.

Roger McGough, who wrote this poem, says it is '*about fathers and sons really*'. The next few questions will help you to examine the father–son relationship more deeply. We can find out a lot about that relationship from the poem, even though only one of the people involved is still alive to say anything about it.

NOW TRY THIS

1. What is it in line 12 that helps us to start working out that the poem is about a father–son relationship?
2. Look at verse 3 of the poem, lines 22–27. The speaker makes three statements in the second part of this verse. Which one of them is true?
3. Which two statements in that verse are not true, even though the speaker believes that they are?
4. The speaker concludes in the last verse that his son was just '*minding*' the cigarettes '*for one of the older boys*.' This seems really trivial when we think of the fact that his son has been killed. Why is it so important to the father to be able to believe this about his son?

NOW TRY THIS

You should discuss the following question with a partner, a group, or with your class. When you have agreed on an answer, make sure everyone writes it down.

■ In what way(s) is the poem '*about fathers and sons*'?

Clichés

A **cliché** is a phrase that begins to seem empty, or even annoying, because it is overused. Many clichés started life as interesting expressions, but overuse has made them dull.

Interviews with football managers are often full of clichés. For example, if the manager says that the match was '*a game of two halves*' or that he is '*over the moon*' with the result, he has used a cliché.

We all use clichés all the time in real life. Often we use them in trivial conversations, when we are just making small talk and don't really have much to say. People also fall into cliché sometimes in very tense or difficult situations. At times like these, simple, familiar words can seem less scary than words that are more powerful, emotional, or descriptive.

NOW TRY THIS

- In line 3, the speaker uses two clichés. What are the two separate clichés he uses?
- Why is he speaking in clichés at this point?

Metaphor

In a **metaphor** a writer suggests that one thing *is* another. This is not true, but it helps the author to make a strong comparison. For example, if we say:

'That boy is a monster.'

we know the boy doesn't really have green fur and long fangs, but when we read this line we understand that there is something about his personality that is monstrous and nasty.

Similarly, if we say:

'That girl is an angel'

we know that the girl being described here does not have wings and a halo, and that she doesn't live on a fluffy cloud playing a harp. By calling her 'an angel' the writer is telling us about her personality. The girl must be kind, good, or well behaved.

Metaphors can be used just to make descriptions more interesting. They can also be used to help us understand what some unusual object is like. They can help us see how a feeling affects the person feeling it, by making a comparison to something we can more easily understand.

NOW TRY THIS

Answer the following questions:

1. In line 10 the speaker uses a metaphor. Quote the metaphor he uses.
2. Which two things are being compared here?
3. How does this same line also help us to feel even more sorry for the victim?

Rhyme

In Chapter 7, on *My Papa's Waltz*, we found that rhyme was used to create a happy mood and to help us understand that the poem was about a happy memory. Roger McGough, the writer of 'The Identification', is certainly not trying to create a happy mood with a poem about such a sad event.

In *My Papa's Waltz* the rhyming words came at the ends of the lines, which is where we would normally expect to find them. McGough sometimes does this but he also uses rhymes tucked into the middles of some of the lines of the poem.

Roethke uses rhyme all the way through his poem. McGough uses only a few rhymes. When he does use rhyme, he must have a special reason for doing so. McGough's rhymes catch our attention and make us look more closely at the lines the rhymes are in. He is using the rhyming words to focus us in on certain lines, so that he can emphasise more strongly what is being seen, or said, or felt in those lines.

NOW TRY THIS

Answer the following questions about the rhymes in the poem.

The first rhyme is in verse 1.

1. Quote the rhyme.
2. Why is he using rhyme here? What effect is he trying to get?

The next rhyme is in verse 2. In fact it is a very clever double rhyme.

3. Quote the rhyme.
4. Why is he using rhyme here? What effect is he trying to get?

The third and last rhyme can be found in verse 5.

5. Quote the rhyme.
6. Why is he using rhyme here? What effect is he trying to get?

There are a couple of other times when McGough uses similar sounding words hidden in the middle of lines in the poem.

7. Look for the hidden rhyme in verse 2. Quote the two lines that contain this hidden rhyme and underline the rhyming words. Why is he using rhyme here? What effect is he trying to get?
8. Look for the hidden rhyme in verse 3. This one is harder to find. Quote the group of three lines that contains this and underline the rhyming words. Why is he using rhyme here? What effect is he trying to get?

Repetition

As we discovered in Chapter 6 *Child on Top of a Greenhouse*, when a poet repeats words, or uses them more often than you would expect in normal speech and writing, there is usually a reason behind this.

NOW TRY THIS

Copy the following table into your notebook and use it to explain why each of these words has been repeated.

Word, verse	Reason
black, v.1	
face, v.2	
pockets, v.4	

Some other techniques

We have already looked at the use of repetition, rhyme, metaphor, cliché and theme in this poem. Now we are going to learn about some other techniques McGough uses, and to find examples of these techniques in the poem.

The following words in **bold** give the names of techniques, and explain what these techniques mean. Then for each one there is a short question about the use of that technique in this poem.

NOW TRY THIS

Read the explanation of each technique. Then answer the questions that follow, in your notebook.

- **Allusion: an indirect reference, a suggestion or a hint**
  Which object belonging to Stephen in verse 3 alludes to a hobby, or a way he spent his free time? State the object and the hobby.

- **Ambivalence: having two different feelings or attitudes about something at the same time**
  Explain the two different feelings or attitudes Stephen's dad has when he sees the scoutbelt.

- **Connotation: all the different meanings and suggestions that go along with something**
  Look at the mention of Stephen's key ring in verse 5.

  1. What is connoted or suggested about his age?
  2. What is connoted or suggested about his relationship with his grandmother?

- **Symbol: a thing that stands for or represents something else**
  In this poem Stephen is dead. In a very important sense he is gone, not there. Some of his possessions act as symbols. They stand for him and the life he had.

  1. Pick out three of his belongings that symbolise Stephen as his dad remembers him.
  2. Which of Stephen's belongings symbolise or stand for the secrets he kept from his dad, or the things his dad didn't know about him?

Another way to look at this poem

You might like to use this as a revision task just before your exam. It will help to get you back into the poem, but give you something fresh to think about at the same time.

So far, we have just assumed that the words of the poem are spoken aloud by the dead boy's father when he comes to identify his son's body. However, it might be the case that some of the words are things the man says, but that others are just words he thinks to himself, and never voices out loud.

NOW TRY THIS

You'll need a photocopy of the next page to do this task. The lines of the poem have been printed here without verse breaks. Read through the poem carefully. When you find a line or a group of lines that you think are the father's thoughts, not his words, draw a think bubble around them. The first one has been done for you.

The Identification

So you think it's Stephen?
Then I'd best make sure.
Be on the safe side as it were.
Ah, there's been a mistake. The hair
you see, it's black, now Stephen's fair...
What's that? The explosion?

Of course, burnt black. Silly of me.
I should have known.

Then let's get on.

The face. Is that a face I ask?
That mask of charred wood,
blistered, scarred – could
that have been a child's face?
The sweater, where intact, looks
in fact all too familiar.
But one must be sure.
The scoutbelt. Yes that's his.
I recognise the studs he hammered in
not a week ago. At the age
when boys get clothes-conscious
now you know. Remove all trace of doubt.
Pull out every splinter of hope.
Pockets. Empty the pockets.
Handkerchief? Could be any schoolboy's.
Dirty enough. Cigarettes?
Oh this can't be Stephen.
I don't allow him to smoke you see.
He wouldn't disobey me, not his father.
But that's his penknife. That's his all right.
And that's his key on the key ring
Gran gave him just the other night.
So this must be him.
I think I know what happened...
about the cigarettes.
No doubt he was minding them
for one of the older boys.
Yes that's it.
That's him.
That's our Stephen.

One more way to think about this poem

This would also make a good revision task. You will need a photocopy of pages 161–162. We know that although only the dead boy's father is talking, there is someone else there, perhaps a doctor or a police officer. You have been given the whole text of the poem. Whenever you see a gap, put in the words you think the police officer is saying – exactly as that person would say them. The first one has been done as an example.

The Identification

So you think it's Stephen?

We're not sure just now, but it could be your son.

Then I'd best make sure.
Be on the safe side as it were.
Ah, there's been a mistake.

The hair you see, it's black, now Stephen's fair…

What's that? The explosion?
Of course, burnt black. Silly of me.
I should have known.

Then let's get on.
The face. Is that a face I ask?
That mask of charred wood,
blistered, scarred – could
that have been a child's face?
The sweater, where intact, looks
in fact all too familiar.
But one must be sure.

The scoutbelt. Yes that's his.
I recognise the studs he hammered in
not a week ago. At the age
when boys get clothes-conscious
now you know. Remove all trace of doubt.

Pull out every splinter of hope.
Pockets. Empty the pockets.

Handkerchief? Could be any schoolboy's.
Dirty enough.

Cigarettes?
Oh this can't be Stephen.

I don't allow him to smoke you see.

He wouldn't disobey me, not his father.

But that's his penknife. That's his all right.
And that's his key on the key ring
Gran gave him just the other night.
So this must be him.

I think I know what happened…
about the cigarettes.
No doubt he was minding them
for one of the older boys.
Yes that's it.
That's him.

That's our Stephen.

Possible essay tasks

Now that you've finished studying this poem, you could tackle the following essay questions. Remember to follow the advice from Chapter 9 on how to write literature essays.

Above the poetry essay choices on the exam paper you'll see the following words:

Answers to questions in this section should refer to such relevant features as: word choice, theme, imagery…

Now look at the essay choices:

■ Choose a poem which describes the feelings of a character.

Say what the feelings are and then go on to show how some of the words or phrases made the feelings clear to you.

or

■ Choose a poem in which there is someone for whom you feel sympathy.

Explain why you feel sympathetic towards the person, and what particular words and phrases the poet has used which make you feel this way.

9 The Critical Essay

The final assessment for the Intermediate 1 course is made up of two short exams which you will sit one day in May.

The first of these is the Close Reading exam, which is dealt with in Chapter 2. The second exam paper is called the Critical Essay.

If you did Standard Grade then you've written Critical Essays before, even if you weren't used to calling them that. The Folio that you sent away to the examiners contained two or three Critical Essays. You may have known them as 'reading essays', or by a number of other names such as 'reading answers' or 'critical responses'. Whatever you call them, in these essays you have to show your knowledge and understanding of a text you have studied. You should also be able to explain some of the ways in which the author achieved what he or she wanted to with that text.

There are several important differences between the way you tackled these essays in Standard Grade and the way you will need to approach them now in Intermediate.

In Standard Grade	In Intermediate
■ You wrote essays to send away in your Folio.	■ You write an essay in the exam.
■ Your Folio contained two or three critical essays.	■ You write just one essay in the exam.
■ You could redraft and rework the essay.	■ You get just one go at writing the essay.
■ Your teacher probably gave you the essay topic.	■ You have to choose a topic from the exam paper.
■ The topic was designed to fit the text you had studied.	■ The essay topics are quite vague.
■ Your teacher may have given you a plan to follow.	■ You have to plan the essay yourself.
■ You could have lots of class time and homework time to work on your essay.	■ You get 45 minutes.
■ You had as much support as you needed from your teacher.	■ You're on your own!

You may have been wondering why you would need a whole chapter in this book to tell you how to write an essay. The lists of differences above may explain why.

If you haven't done Standard Grade you can probably still see why the Intermediate 1 Critical Essay is a tougher challenge than any essay you have written in the past.

Why do the examiners want you to write an essay? What do they want you to prove about your skills?

They are actually looking at four different areas of your essay-writing skill: **understanding**, **analysis**, **evaluation** and **expression**.

- ■ **Understanding** means how well you understand and know the text you have studied.

- ■ **Analysis** means being able to examine the way the writer writes and the techniques he or she uses.

- ■ **Evaluation** means having a personal response to and a personal opinion about what you have read.

- ■ **Expression** is how well you use the English language in your writing. This includes your spelling, grammar and punctuation.

Let's start by looking at how the Critical Essay exam paper is organised. It comes in the form of a four-page booklet.

- The front page has the name and date of the exam, and tells you the start and finish times. It will also remind you to 'Answer **one** question only', for which you can earn up to 25 marks.

- The middle pages contain the essay choices.

Choosing an essay

Obviously the bit we are most interested in lies in the centre pages, where the essay choices are. This may look a little different from some of the past papers you may see at school because the layout of the paper changed in 2006. At the top of that page you'll find a general instruction like this:

The following will be assessed:

- **the relevance of your essay to the question you have chosen**

- **your understanding of the main points of the text(s) through some reference to the relevant areas of content**

- **your explanation of the ways in which aspects of structure/style/language contribute to the meaning/effect/impact of the chosen text(s)**

- **your personal reaction to the content or style of the text(s) supported by some textual reference**

- **the quality and technical accuracy of your writing.**

This is all just another way of telling you about the skills the examiners are assessing.

The essay choices are divided into five sections from A to E, like this:

- Section A – Drama

- Section B – Prose

- Section C – Poetry

- Section D – Film and TV Drama

- Section E – Language

At the start of each section you will see specific advice for that type of essay. We will find out more about that later in this chapter.

Very few schools in Scotland prepare their pupils to write about Film and TV Drama and even fewer encourage their pupils to study for the Language option. Most pupils sitting Intermediate study a mixture of poetry, plays, short stories and novels. You can write about plays in the Drama section. The short stories and novels you learn about in class are Prose. Since all the texts in this book are poems or short stories, all the examples from now on will come from the Poetry and Prose sections of the exam papers. This is just so that we can base our examples on work you will find in other parts of this book. The techniques you will learn should help you, though, to write about any kind of written text that you have studied this year.

Under each of the five headings you will see two essay choices. That means that if you have studied one play, one piece of prose and one poem then there will be six possible essays for you to choose from. But remember, you only have to write one! How are you going to make your choice?

To begin to work this out, we need to look at the way the questions are worded. All the essay tasks follow the same pattern. They are set out in two paragraphs. Here's an essay task from a recent exam:

> **Choose a novel, or a short story, which has an important turning point that changes things for one of the characters.**
>
> **Show how the story builds up to the turning point and say why it is important for the character.**

So how are you going to choose which essay to write? You're going to look at just the **first paragraph** of the essay topic.

As soon as you see these words, you need to ask yourself a few questions. Let's assume you go into the exam knowing all the stories and poems in this book. You can ask yourself:

Have I studied a novel?

To which the answer would be:

No.

That doesn't mean you have to rule out trying this essay. The next thing you need to ask yourself is:

Have I studied any short stories?

This time the answer is:

Yes, three of them: *Snakes and Ladders, Kid in a Bin*, **and** *Lamb to the Slaughter.*

So, you **might** be able to write this essay. Now it's time to focus in even tighter on that first paragraph and look at **what kind of short story** the examiners want you to write about.

which has an important turning point that changes things for one of the characters.

So now you need to ask yourself:

> **Is there a turning point in any of these stories, a point where things change for one of the characters?**

This essay question turns out to be quite a good one, because you get three quite positive answers:

> **In *Snakes and Ladders* Lily doesn't manage to persuade the council to give her a new flat, so she decides to set light to her home.**

> **In *Kid in a Bin* Anthony's mother dies of skin cancer so he decides to stay away from the sun by hiding inside a bin.**

> **In *Lamb to the Slaughter* Mary's husband tells her he is going to leave her, and she snaps and kills him with a leg of lamb.**

It's time to narrow down your choice. To help you do this, take another look at the words in **the second paragraph** of the task. This paragraph is where the examiners tell you how they actually want you to tackle the essay. The words of the second paragraph give you instructions that you must follow. If you don't obey the instructions in paragraph 2 of the task, you aren't answering the essay question and you will certainly not pass.

For this essay, these words in paragraph 2 are important.

Now you can narrow down your options by asking yourself:

Are there any of the stories that don't really build up to the turning point?

This allows you to think:

I can rule out *Kid In A Bin* because Anthony's mother died before the start of the story, and when the story begins he's already living in the bin. That story doesn't really build up to the turning point.

You could still write about either of the other stories. In *Snakes and Ladders* the story builds up to the turning point by letting us see what happens when Lily goes to the housing office for her interview with the clerk. In *Lamb to the Slaughter* the story builds up to the turning point by showing us how contented and happy Mary is at home, and how Patrick destroys all of that by telling her that he plans to leave. At this stage you can choose which essay to write by asking yourself:

Which story do I know better?

Which one have I revised more carefully?

Which one do I think I could write about better?

Or you could carry on looking through the relevant sections of the exam paper until you find a different essay that appeals to you even more.

NOW TRY THIS

Below you will see just the first paragraph from a number of essays taken from old exam papers. All of them could be used to get you to write about at least one of the stories or poems in this book. Some of them could fit more than one text.

For each one, decide which text or texts you could base the essay on. (If you have studied other texts in class that are not included in this book, you can try to find essays to match those texts too.)

1. Choose a novel or a short story which deals with a crisis in a family or a community.
2. Choose a novel or a short story or a piece of non-fiction or a group of prose texts which interests you because it deals with young people.
3. Choose a poem about an incident or an event.
4. Choose a poem which describes the feelings of a character.
5. Choose a novel or a short story which has a surprise ending.
6. Choose a novel or a short story or a piece of non-fiction or a group of prose texts which interests you because of its theme or topic.
7. Choose a poem about a person or an animal or a place.
8. Choose a poem which seems to you to deal with unhappiness.
9. Choose a poem which focuses on a person's experience.
10. Choose a poem which creates a particular mood or atmosphere for you.

Writing your introduction

The first paragraph you write in the essay will be your introduction. Whenever you write a literature essay, the same three things should appear in the introduction:

1. the title of the text you read

2. the name of the author who wrote this text

3. a clear indication of what you will be writing about.

As we've already seen, the first paragraph of the essay task helps you to choose which task you are going to do. Once you have chosen an essay to tackle, that same first paragraph of the task instructions is also useful for something else. It helps you to write the introduction to your essay. To do this, you are going to **recycle** many of the words from that paragraph.

For example, let's assume that you have chosen to do the essay task we looked at in detail earlier, and that you are going to write about *Snakes and Ladders*. Here's the first paragraph from the essay task we saw earlier on and thought about so carefully. Look at the words printed in **bold** type.

We are going to recycle all of those words in the introduction to the essay. Those words help you to give a clear indication of what you will be writing about. You still need to add the title and author to these to have a complete introduction. Your introduction would end up looking like this:

A short story which has an important turning point that changes things for one of the characters is 'Snakes and Ladders' by Dilys Rose.

Can you see the words that have been recycled from the task instructions?

Now go back and look at the long list of opening paragraphs of essay tasks printed on page 171. As it happens, the first paragraph on that list can also lead you into writing an essay about *Snakes and Ladders*. That paragraph said this:

Choose a novel or a short story which deals with a crisis in a family or a community.

So your introduction this time would look like this:

One short story which deals with a crisis in a family is 'Snakes and Ladders' by Dilys Rose.

Again, look for the words that have been recycled from the task instructions.

NOW TRY THIS

Look back at that whole list of opening paragraphs from essay instructions on page 171. Can you turn each one into the introduction to an essay? Every one of them suits at least one of the texts that you can find and study in this book.

The summary paragraph

After the introduction, it's a good idea to write a **short** summary of your text. Any teacher can choose to teach his or her class any texts that they enjoy, and that they think their class will like. This means that you may end up writing your Critical Essay about a text that the exam marker has never read, or maybe even never heard of. Writing a **short** summary will give the marker a little bit of context and background, making it easier for him or her to understand comments you make about that text in your essay.

Take care! You'll have noticed that bold type is used twice to remind you that you should be writing a **short** summary. The summary itself does not earn you any marks. It just helps you and the exam marker to get your heads clear. You must not waste precious exam time by waffling.

To let you see what is meant by a **short** summary, here's one for *Snakes and Ladders*:

In this story Lily visits the council housing office to ask for a transfer to a different area. She gets little help from the council clerk and decides to take matters into her own hands by burning down her flat.

That summary is just 40 words long. It should be possible to summarise most texts in fewer than 50 words.

NOW TRY THIS

Read the following summaries. They are both for texts you can read and study in this book. Which text is being summarised in each case?

1. In this story Mary Maloney kills her husband with a leg of frozen lamb because he tells her that he is going to leave her. She then covers up her crime by getting the police to eat the roasted murder weapon.
2. A father who has come to identify the body of his son speaks in this poem. He is at first sure that the dead boy cannot be Stephen, but is gradually shown convincing evidence.

NOW TRY THIS

There are three more texts in this book that have not been summarised. Can you write summaries of those texts in 50 words or less?

The main body of your essay

Once you've written the introduction and summary, it's time for the main body of your essay. This main body will be made up of several paragraphs – four or five will be enough.

We've already looked very carefully at the fact that the first paragraph of the essay instructions tells you what sort of text to write about. The second paragraph of the essay instructions tells you **what you are actually going to do** in your essay. Remember, if you don't do what that second paragraph tells you to do then you aren't answering the question and you will never pass the exam. Here is the second paragraph of that essay which we decided could suit *Snakes and Ladders*:

Show how the story builds up to the turning point and say why it is important for the character.

If you look at this instruction carefully, you will see that in this essay you have two main things to do:

1. Show how the story builds up to the turning point.

2. Say why the turning point is important for the character who faces it.

In fact almost all of the Critical Essays you will find in past papers or in the exam give you two things to do.

NOW TRY THIS

You are going to see the first paragraphs of some essay instructions which you have seen before. This time you will also see the second paragraphs of the instructions. From each second paragraph, pick out the two things you have to do in the main body of the essay.

Choose a novel or a short story which has a surprise ending.
    Briefly say what happens in the story and then go on to show why the surprise ending makes a good finish to the story.

I have to…

Then I have to…

Choose a novel or a short story or a piece of non-fiction or a group of prose texts which interests you because of its theme or topic.
    Say what the theme or topic is and show how the writer makes it interesting for you.

I have to…

Then I have to…

Choose a poem which seems to you to deal with unhappiness.
    Say what the poem is about and then go on to show how some of the words or phrases emphasise the unhappiness.

I have to…

Then I have to…

Choose a poem which focuses on a person's experience.
    Say what that experience is and how the particular words and phrases the poet uses help you to understand how the person feels.

I have to…

Then I have to…

So, now that you know what you are supposed to do, how are you going to do it? Let's take another look at the second, instructing, paragraph in the essay task that we thought would be good for *Snakes and Ladders*. The words telling you what to do have been picked out here in bold.

> **Show how** the story builds up to the turning point and **say why** it is important for the character.

A good way to tackle this essay is to write a couple of paragraphs dealing with the first main thing, looking at how the story builds up to the turning point. Then you could write a couple of paragraphs saying why the turning point is important for Lily. As you write these paragraphs:

■ every one of the main body paragraphs must help you to do what your chosen task tells you to do

■ every one of the main body paragraphs must use evidence from the text.

NOW TRY THIS

Below is an example of a paragraph which does the two things mentioned above. Read it carefully and decide:

1. Does this paragraph come from the 'Show how ...' section of the essay or from the, 'Say why ...' section?
2. Which words in the paragraph show that this pupil is trying to stick to the chosen task?
3. Which words in the paragraph show the pupil is using evidence from the text?

The answers are at the end of the paragraph. Don't look at them until you have worked them out for yourself.

One way that Lily builds up to the turning point of deciding to set fire to her flat is that when she is walking home by the canal she notices something important:

'On the path, the broken bottle had started a small fire.'

I think that this makes her notice how easily fires can start, even without a person being involved. Perhaps she thinks she could start a fire in her flat without anybody realising that she is responsible.

Did you manage to answer the three questions?

1. This paragraph comes from the 'Show how …' section of the essay.

2. The words in the paragraph that show this pupil is trying to stick to the chosen task are:

    One way that Lily builds up to the turning point of deciding to set fire to her flat is that…

3. The words in the paragraph that show the pupil is using evidence from the text are:

    'On the path, the broken bottle had started a small fire.'

Did you notice that this pupil once again recycled some words from the original essay question to help structure his paragraph?

The words *builds up to the turning point* are taken straight from the wording of the task.

Let's focus a bit more carefully on how to write the paragraphs in the main body of your essay. There are two things you should do in these paragraphs so that they will be well written and help you to achieve the task you've chosen.

1. You should begin the paragraph with a **topic sentence**.

2. You should use the **PEE structure**.

Topic sentences are called topic sentences for two reasons. Firstly, they tie in with the topic of your essay. Secondly, they let the reader understand the topic of the paragraph you're on. Using a topic sentence at the start of the paragraph sets you off in the right direction.

NOW TRY THIS

You're going to see again the four essay tasks you examined a few pages ago. After the four tasks you'll see a list of sentences. Each one is a topic sentence which belongs in one of the four essays. Can you decide which essay each topic sentence belongs to?

Here are the **essay topics**:

One   Choose a novel or a short story which has a surprise ending.

Briefly say what happens in the story and then go on to show why the surprise ending makes a good finish to the story.

Two   Choose a novel or a short story or a piece of non-fiction or a group of prose texts which interests you because of its theme or topic.

Say what the theme or topic is and show how the writer makes it interesting for you.

Three   Choose a poem which seems to you to deal with unhappiness.

Say what the poem is about and then go on to show how some of the words or phrases emphasise the unhappiness.

Four   Choose a poem which focuses on a person's experience.

Say what that experience is and how the particular words and phrases the poet uses help you to understand how the person feels.

Here are the **topic sentences**. Can you match each one to the right essay topic?

a) One way the writer emphasises the father's unhappiness is by showing us his inner thoughts as well as his words.

b) The poet helps me understand how the boy feels by having him repeat certain words.

c) One way the writer makes the topic of poverty interesting is by clearly showing us how horrible Lily's neighbourhood is.

d) One way the ending makes a good finish to the story is because we see how clever Mary has been.

e) A word which helps me understand how the boy feels is '*romped*'.

f) Carter makes the topic of families interesting by showing that no family is perfect.

The **PEE structure** helps you to remember what should be in each paragraph.

P – tells you to make a **Point** which is relevant to your essay topic.

E – tells you to give **Evidence** from the text by quoting from or by referring to the text.

E – tells you to **Explain** the effect of this, to show what the writer is doing to us.

The **P** part of this is also the topic sentence of the paragraph, so there's a bit of an overlap between the idea of using a topic sentence, and the idea of following the **PEE structure**.

NOW TRY THIS

Copy the following paragraph into your notebook. Once you've copied it out do these three things:

1. Underline the **Point** part with a straight line.
2. Underline the **Evidence** part with a wiggly or jagged line.
3. Draw a box a round the **Explain** part.

One way the ending makes a good finish to the story is because we see how clever Mary has been. The policemen are still looking for the murder weapon which they think must be

> *'right under our very noses.'*

It is, but only because they are eating it. Mary manages to talk them into eating the leg of lamb. By doing this she gets them to destroy the murder weapon and ruin any evidence that might go against her.

By the way, did you also spot how the pupil placed his quotation so that it would stand out? It is **indented**, set in from the edges of the page to make it narrower than the rest of the essay. If you are quoting anything longer than just a single word or short phrase it is a good idea to **indent**. It lets the marker see that you are using words from the text confidently.

Writing about techniques

This is where that advice above each set of essay tasks comes in. The wording of this paragraph follows a pattern.

NOW TRY THIS

To get you to spot the pattern of this paragraph in the essay instructions, you're going to see the advice for two different types of essay. The first one is for poetry essays, the second one is for prose essays. Read the two paragraphs and then answer the two questions below.

> **Answers to questions in this section should refer to such relevant features as: word choice, theme, imagery...**

> **Answers to questions in this section should refer to such relevant features as: content, character, theme, imagery...**

1. Which words are always used at the **start** of the advice above the essay tasks?
2. What will you always find at the **end** of the advice above the essay tasks?

What this paragraph of advice does is just remind you to write about some of the techniques the author uses, or some of the things that made that text worth studying in the first place.

It doesn't even actually matter which techniques and features you write about. You don't have to write about the ones named in the paragraph, because the three dots at the end of that paragraph allow you to write about whichever techniques and features you think are important for the text and task you have chosen.

For example, if you were writing an essay on *Snakes and Ladders*, depending which essay you chose you could pick any of the following techniques and features which we looked at as we studied the story:

character – Lily or the clerk	*formal language*
use of numbers and sums	*sympathy – for Lily or the clerk*
implication	*setting*
contrast	*personification*
word choice	*theme*
using other people's words	

You don't have to name a technique in every one of your body paragraphs. Doing it once or twice will be enough – it's still more important to make sure that every paragraph you write is tied into your chosen task and helps you to answer the question. You just have to pick up and deal with a couple of techniques on your way through the essay as you answer the question. Also, every time you write about something the author does, you are dealing with technique. Not all features have simple one- or two-word names that you can learn, but if you can say what the writer is doing, and back that up with an example, then you **are** writing about '*relevant features*'.

NOW TRY THIS

You might want to work with a partner or group to do this. You should be quite familiar with this essay task by now. Can you think of:

- two more ways that *Snakes and Ladders* builds up to the turning point
- two reasons why this turning point is important?

Compare your answers with those from the rest of the class. Agree on the best two answers for building each main area of the essay.

NOW TRY THIS

Again, your teacher may let you work with a partner to do this. Look at the two ways and two reasons you agreed on above. Now turn each one into a paragraph for this essay.

Remember to use evidence from the text. If that evidence is in quotations rather than just examples, remember to indent the words that you quote. Also make sure you start with a topic sentence, and be sure that topic sentence works as the **P** part of the **PEE structure** in your paragraph.

Read your paragraphs aloud in class or give them to your teacher for marking.

The conclusion

After your introduction, summary, and main body, you need to finish off your essay with a conclusion. The conclusion needs to do two things:

1. sum up and round off what you have written

2. give your personal response.

Summing up just means reminding the examiner what you have written about. It could be something like this:

In this essay I have shown how the story 'Snakes and Ladders' builds up to a turning point, and said why that turning point is important for Lily, the main character.

Giving your personal response takes a little more thought. Earlier in your school career your personal responses were probably a bit like this:

I liked the story because the writer made me feel sorry for Lily but I did not like the clerk at the council office because he was unhelpful.

You have to do something a little more complicated now, because at Intermediate level your personal response, just like everything else in your essay, should fit your chosen task, as well as fitting the text you are writing about.

This task was about a turning point, so your personal response should say something about what you thought of that turning point, when Lily decides to set fire to her flat. You could say whether you thought that turning point seemed realistic, or how you felt about Lily making that decision. Here's one example of how a pupil tackled it.

The turning point is when she decides to set fire to her flat. This is a really unusual thing to do, but I thought the writer actually made this seem quite realistic. This was because I understood that Lily could not think of any other way things could change. I felt very sorry for her and I wondered if she would really do it and whether her plan would work.

So, that's it. You know how to write an essay. If you've worked through this chapter you have found out, step by step, how to tackle this part of the exam. Before you go into the exam, your teacher will give you lots of chances to practise essay writing in class.

NOW TRY THIS

You're going to see the whole of the wording for that *Snakes and Ladders* essay again. This time it will be followed by a paragraph plan to help you build up a whole essay in seven paragraphs.

First of all, above the essay choices for prose the exam paper has this wording:

> Answers to questions in this section should refer to such relevant features as: content, character, theme, imagery...

Then you see this essay task:

> Choose a novel, or a short story, which has an important turning point that changes things for one of the characters.

> Show how the story builds up to the turning point and say why it is important for the character.

Follow the plan to write the essay.

Para 1 Here's the introduction you saw earlier in this chapter. You can copy it out and use it in your essay:

> A short story which has an important turning point that changes things for one of the characters is 'Snakes and Ladders' by Dilys Rose.

Para 2 Here's the summary you saw earlier in this chapter. You can copy it out and use it in your essay:

> In this story Lily visits the council housing office to ask for a transfer to a different area. She gets little help from the council clerk and decides to take matters into her own hands by burning down her flat.

Paras 3, 4, 5, 6 For each of these paragraphs, the topic sentence is provided for you. Copy it out. Then complete each paragraph, remembering to stick to the question and to use evidence from the text. Remember to use the **PEE structure** for each paragraph.

> 3 One way that the story builds up to the turning point is by showing us that Lily does not get much help from the council clerk.
>
> 4 Another way that the story builds up towards the turning point is that Lily notices how nasty her estate is compared with the nicer houses nearby.
>
> 5 This turning point is important for Lily because she is taking charge when usually things just happen to her.
>
> 6 This turning point is also important for Lily because starting the fire could go well or it could go badly.

Para 7 This is your conclusion. You can use the same summing up you saw before. Here it is:

> In this essay I have shown how the story 'Snakes and Ladders' builds up to a turning point, and said why that turning point is important for Lily, the main character.

Now you have to write your own personal response. What did **you** think of the turning point in this story? Write it now to finish off your essay.

Check over your essay and then hand it in to your teacher for marking.

NOW TRY THIS

Much earlier on in the chapter, we discovered that another essay on that original list would also fit *Snakes and Ladders* quite well. Here is the task for it:

> Choose a novel or a short story which deals with a crisis in a family or a community.

> Briefly say what happens in the story, and then go on to show how the family, or the community, deals with the crisis.

Remember that above that task on the exam paper is the advice reminding you to write about relevant features and techniques.

Can you follow the principles you've learned in this chapter to write **this** essay? Your teacher may let you do the planning in a pair, in a group, or with the whole class.

10 | The Personal Study

What you have to do

The Personal Study is one of the four assessments, often called NABs, which you have to pass in school before going on to sit the final exam. For this assessment you have to choose a literature text to study. This will often be a whole book, though you could study a poem, or a few poems, or a short story. Then you have to write an essay, the Personal Study, about your chosen text.

What the examiners are looking for

Why do the examiners want you to write your Personal Study? What do they want you to prove about your skills?

They are actually looking at four different areas of your skill: **understanding, analysis, evaluation** and **expression**.

- **Understanding** What you write must show that you understand the main points of your chosen text. You should refer to parts of the text that are relevant to the topic you've chosen.

- **Analysis** You should examine the writer's structure, style or language. You need to show how these contribute to the meaning, or effect, or impact of the text you have studied.

- **Evaluation** You must show a personal response to or a personal opinion about the text you have read. Your response should be supported by evidence.

- **Expression** The marker should be able to follow your line of thought through the Study. You should use the English language well and clearly in your writing. This includes your spelling, grammar and punctuation.

I must be sure to use good ~~speling~~ spelling and ~~punktution~~ punctuation.

What makes this task challenging

The Personal Study is one of the most challenging tasks you will have to work on in Intermediate 1. It's hard work because of the level of independence asked of you:

■ You have to choose your own text.

■ You have to read it by yourself, and probably in your own time.

■ You have to make your own notes about the text.

■ You have to work out what makes the text worth studying.

■ You have to choose your own task and title.

■ You have to plan the Study by yourself.

■ You have to write and check over the Study for yourself before you hand it in.

Building on what you already know

The list above might sound very daunting. However, if you think about it another way, the Personal Study is just another literature essay. It's a good idea not to try to produce your Personal Study until after you have written a couple of literature essays about texts that you have studied in class. If you wait until then, many of the things that make the Personal Study seem hard will actually come quite naturally to you.

There are some things you need to do in the Personal Study that you don't have to do when you write other literature essays:

■ For this NAB you have to choose your own text – in other literature essays you will be writing about a text that your teacher chose for your class to study.

- For this NAB you have to make up your own title — in other literature essays you will be writing to fit a task from an exam paper.

- For this NAB you have to work out what makes the text worth studying — in other literature essays you will be writing about things your teacher has taught you about the text.

Despite all this, the Personal Study is basically just another literature essay. All the things you have learned about how to write one of these essays still apply. The Personal Study will follow the same pattern and structure that you are learning to use for other essays:

- There will be an introduction in which you name the author and title and explain what you will be writing about.

- There will be a brief summary paragraph to give a flavour of the text.

- The main body of the essay will have about four or five paragraphs that fit the task or title you have chosen.

- You will show that these paragraphs fit the task by starting each one with a good topic sentence.

- In those body paragraphs you will use the PEE structure.

- Your Personal Study will end with a conclusion and personal response that fits your chosen task.

If all of that is familiar and makes sense then you must already have had some experience in writing literature essays, and you're probably ready to have a go at your Personal Study.

If it's not familiar then you aren't ready yet to write your Personal Study. However, you can still do something very important to prepare for the Personal Study. You can choose a text.

Choosing a text

What kind of text to choose (and avoid)

You shouldn't write your Personal Study about a text anyone has taught you before. If you did this, it wouldn't be your own Personal Study, but just another literature essay.

You should choose a text where the writer is trying to create a good piece of literature as well as just tell a cracking story. Your teacher will be able to help you spot the difference.

You should almost certainly choose something written for adult readers. You'll find *Northern Lights* and *The Curious Incident of the Dog in the Night-Time* listed later on in this chapter, and they were written for younger audiences. They have what's called 'crossover appeal' because adults enjoy them too. They are also both very well written, and have definite literary merit. In most cases, though, anything written for children or younger readers will not have enough in it for you to analyse.

You need to be very careful with certain books. Most examples of what we call **genre fiction** are unsuitable. These include most books in the thriller genre, most books in the detective genre, most books in the romance genre, most horror books, and most of the books aimed at young woman readers and often called 'chick lit'. Writers of genre fiction tend to focus very much on plot. They often have quite simple themes, and the same types of characters crop up in book after book. As with books for younger readers, there are sometimes examples of genre fiction that can be studied for this NAB. Although Stephen King is best known as a horror writer, one or two of his other works are appropriate for your Personal Study, and you'll find them listed later on in this chapter. Also on that list is Ian Rankin, a Scottish writer whose books are about an Edinburgh detective called Inspector Rebus. Rankin's novels are very high quality and have lots you can examine.

You also need to take care with books that tell real-life stories. A book in which a writer describes someone else's life is called **biography**. One in which a person writes his or her own life story is called an **autobiography**. **A memoir** is a book in which someone tells us about a particular event or time in their life.

These books are often really interesting to read. However, they are often not very well written. If someone is very famous for something they have done, like being a pop star or a sports star, they may have an interesting life story to tell. They may also have a host of fans who will pay a lot of money to read about that life. However, someone who is famous for football or singing has probably spent all their time becoming good at that, and is unlikely to be a good and stylish writer too. There probably won't be enough in their book for you to analyse and be critical about.

Sometimes these people don't even write the story themselves. Even if the star's own name is on the cover, a paid author, called a 'ghost writer', may have written it for them, so the book is pretending to be something it isn't, which again makes it hard for you to analyse.

Biographies written about people who are already very famous can often be even worse than autobiographies. They may be written just to get money from fans, and are frequently made up of material from old interviews or news articles.

Some autobiographies and memoirs *are* well written. This tends to happen most when the book is about the life of someone who is not famous already. Publishers will only spend money producing a book like that if they think it is stylish and people will want to read it. You will find recommendations of some of these books later in this chapter.

Even then, you have to be careful. You do get some autobiographies and memoirs by previously unknown writers which are still not worthy of study. In the last few years many top-selling books have dealt with abusive childhoods – books like those by Dave Pelzer or Julie Gregory. They are gripping (and a bit horrifying) to read, but they aren't stylishly written.

There's one more thing to take care about. If you do choose a well-written autobiography or memoir, you should steer clear of writing about the main character. When the main character is also the writer, it's hard for that person to be honest and objective about himself or herself. They may not give a full picture of what they are like. You can still choose a book like this, but it's better to stick to writing about something else like a theme, or an aspect of the writer's style.

So now that we've looked at the sorts of texts you shouldn't study, how will you find one you could study?

Where to get recommendations

There are lots of people who might be able to help you choose a text. Ask friends or family members about anything they have enjoyed and why they thought it was good. Staff at your local library or your school librarian may be able to suggest texts. They'll be able to do this better if you explain why you need to choose a text and what you're going to do with it. Your teacher may be able to take your whole class to a library to give you time to choose. This can be very useful, because if the teacher knows you well he or she may be able to suggest texts they know you'd like. Or, if you find a text that seems interesting, your teacher should be able to take a look at it and let you know if it's suitable.

You could also make a shopping trip. Lots of big supermarkets sell books nowadays, but when you're looking for a book for your Personal Study you'll need to go to a specialist book store, somewhere like Waterstone's, Borders or Ottaker's. These shops carry thousands of different books. Take time to browse around and see what interests you.

You could also think about things you have enjoyed reading in the past. You might want to try a text by an author whose work you have enjoyed before. You might want to find a text that fits into a genre that you know you like.

If you find yourself picking a book up it's probably because you liked the cover, or the title, or because you recognised the name of the author. What should you do next?

- Read the blurb on the back. If it sounds interesting, go on to the next step. If not, put the book back and look for another one.

- Now open the book. Read the first couple of pages. If they sound interesting, go on to the next step. If not, put the book back and look for another one.

■ It's time to get comfortable. Sit down somewhere and read the first chapter, or the first ten pages. If you still like the book by this time, then it may well be the right book for you to study. If not, start again and look for another book.

So far we've mostly used the word 'book' for what you'll be reading. However, from now on we'll mostly call it a 'text' because it doesn't actually have to be a whole book at all. If you feel you're not up to reading a whole book in the way this NAB demands, it's totally acceptable to write about a short story, or to compare a couple of short stories instead. Most school English departments have books of short stories, so you could start by asking your teacher for advice. If you've read and liked the stories in this book by Roald Dahl and Dilys Rose, you might want to find out about the many other stories these writers have produced. Two other good short story writers (who also happen to be Scottish) are Brian McCabe and Alan Spence.

Some suggestions

Below is just a brief list of some whole books that might be suitable for your Intermediate 1 Personal Study.

Author and title	Summary	You might study...
Adams, Douglas *The Hitch Hiker's Guide to the Galaxy*	Arthur is rescued from Earth, just before it is destroyed, by his friend who turns out to be an alien.	...Arthur – if he's the last remaining human, what is the author saying about human nature through the main character?
Arnott, Jake *The Long Firm*	Novel about a 1960s gangster, Harry Stark. Each chapter is told by a different character who knew him.	...Harry's character – is he just a violent bully or does he have a good side too?
Barker, Pat *Regeneration*	Novel set in the First World War, based on the real life of poet Wilfred Owen.	...the theme of war, or the different ways that war affects different characters.
Brookmyre, Christopher *A Big Boy Did It And Ran Away*	Funny and exciting Scottish novel about a teacher who ends up fighting a terrorist.	...what makes the book funny. You could also look at how it is quite different from most thrillers.

Author and title	Summary	You might study...
Doherty, Berlie *Dear Nobody*	Teenage pregnancy, told from the point of view of both young parents.	...the contrast between Chris and Helen, or the differences between their families, or the way Helen's attitude to her baby changes throughout the pregnancy.
Doyle, Roddy *The Woman Who Walked Into Doors*	Paula deals with her violent husband, her four children, and her own heavy drinking.	...Paula's character. How do her strengths and weaknesses help her to deal with her problems, or even cause them in the first place?
Freud, Esther *Hideous Kinky*	The narrator and her sister are taken to live in Morocco by their hippy mother.	...how the writer makes the story seem to come from a child's point of view, or you could look at the contrast between the narrator and her sister.
Golding, William *Lord of the Flies*	A group of schoolboys wrecked on a deserted island try to cope but end up trying to kill each other.	...the contrast between the two main characters, or the theme of the evil to be found in human nature.
Haddon, Mark *The Curious Incident of the Dog in the Night-Time*	15-year-old autistic Christopher solves a murder mystery and learns about his family and himself.	...how Christopher changes, or how he copes with challenges, or some of the features of the way he tells his story.
Hill, Susan *I'm the King of the Castle*	Rivalry and violence between step brothers.	...the contrast between the two boys, or the ways their relationship develops and changes.
Lee, Harper *To Kill a Mockingbird*	Racism and prejudice in 1930s America, told from a child's point of view.	...the theme of prejudice and misunderstanding, or you could examine one of the main characters.

Author and title	Summary	You might study...
King, Stephen *The Body* (this short novel is part of a longer book called *Different Seasons*)	A group of boys head off to look for a dead body in the woods. This novel was filmed as *Stand By Me*.	...the contrasting characters of the boys in the group, or what they learn on their journey.
King, Stephen *The Shawshank Redemption* (this short novel is part of a longer book called *Different Seasons*)	Andy spends nearly 30 years in prison, but is innocent and eventually escapes.	...Andy's character, or how the prison environment brings out different qualities in different people.
Orwell, George *Animal Farm*	Animals rise up against their master, but their fairer farm soon becomes just as unfair.	...what the writer is trying to say about humans and human society by using animal characters.
Pullman, Philip *Northern Lights*	In a world like but unlike Britain, Lyra searches for a lost friend, meeting witches, armoured bears and evil humans on the way.	...Pullman's creation of a setting and how he makes it like but unlike a place we can recognise.
Rankin, Ian Inspector Rebus novels – you might want to start with the first one, *Knots and Crosses*	Rebus solves crimes in Edinburgh, often in conflict with his colleagues and fighting his own problems of drink, loneliness and broken relationships.	...the character of Rebus – he's a very complex man with both good and bad qualities.
Salinger, J. D. *The Catcher in the Rye*	Holden describes how being expelled from school led to a series of adventures in New York and eventual nervous breakdown.	...Holden's character, or his relationships with other people.
Sebold, Alice *The Lovely Bones*	Murder victim watches from Heaven as her family and friends deal with her death.	...the theme of grief and how different people react differently to it.

Author and title	Summary	You might study...
Spark, Muriel *The Prime of Miss Jean Brodie*	Study of a school teacher and the influence she has on her pupils.	...is Miss Brodie a hero or a villain, a good influence or a bad one?
Swofford, Anthony *Jarhead*	American marine tells us about his time at war in Iraq.	...the themes of violence and anger, and why these are still important even when there is no warfare going on.
Syal, Meera Anita and Me	Meena, the only Indian child in town, becomes friends with, but eventually grows out of the lively Anita.	...the theme of racism, or how Meena gradually begins to se what Anita is like, or the contrast between the two girls.

You have to choose a text that you like, because you'll be spending a lot of time reading it and working on it. Once you've found something you think you are going to like, make sure you check with your teacher to see if it's suitable. There's no point wasting your time doing a lot of reading if you can't use that text in the end. Don't go on any further with your study until you know from your teacher that what you've chosen is appropriate.

After your teacher has agreed that you've made a good choice, you should make sure you have your own copy of the text. There are two reasons for this. First, you're going to need your text for a long time – too long to borrow it from a library. More importantly, if the text is yours, you can mark it. You can underline or highlight useful bits you'd like to quote from. You can write notes in the margin. You can turn back the corners of pages to remind you that that's where important sections are. That way, when you write your final Study you can use just the text and your plan to help you. You won't need to have piles of notes all over your desk. In fact, you're not meant to use piles of notes when you write the final study – just your plan and the book. That's why you need to make the text work for you.

Choosing a title

Once you do have a suitable text, you need to work out which aspect of it you are going to study. To be able to do this you need to get to know the text really well. It's time for some reading and notemaking.

Making basic notes

You may end up reading your chosen text more than once. The first time you read it you'll be doing so in a fairly general way. By the end of this reading you need a good outline – what happens, who the characters are, how they relate to each other. At the end of this reading you also need to be able to choose an angle for your study.

As you read right through the text for the first time you're going to do these three things:

1. Make notes on a piece of paper after every five pages (or after every chapter if the chapters are very short) about what's happening. If your text is a short story, make notes after each page.

2. Circle the name of each character the first time he or she is introduced.

3. Highlight or underline any important quotations you think you might want to use later – these might be things characters say, or parts of the storytelling.

NOW TRY THIS

Take a look at the example below. The pupil is reading *Hideous Kinky* by Esther Freud, one of the books on the list of suggestions. Here are the pupil's written notes. This book has short chapters, so the pupil has made a note after every chapter.

Ch 1   *The narrator describes the trip to Morocco with her mum and sister and her mum's friends, and how they get turned back the first time they try to cross the border.*

Ch 2   *After a wait because the van breaks down, the family get to the city of Marrakech and find a house to rent.*

Ch 3   *The children begin to explore the city, buying local clothes, eating food from the market and going to the steam baths.*

At the same time as making these written notes, the pupil also circled names of characters the first time they appeared, and underlined quotations she thought might be useful. Whenever she underlined a quotation she wrote in the margin of the book to remind herself why she thought the words might be useful.

NOW TRY THIS

Look at the first page of the novel. Can you see how the pupil marked the text?

** *Why doesn't he want his own wife to come with them? What's going on between him and the narrator's mother?*

CHAPTER ONE

It wasn't until we were halfway through France that we noticed Maretta wasn't talking. She sat very still in the back of the van and watched us all with bright eyes.

I crawled across the mattress to her. "Maretta, will you tell us a story?"

Maretta sighed and turned her head away.

* John was doing the driving. He was driving fast with one hand * on the wheel. John was Maretta's husband. He had brought her along at the last minute only because, I heard him tell my mother, she wasn't well.

Bea glared at me.

"Maretta . . . " I began again dutifully, but Maretta placed her light white hand on the top of my head and held it there until my skull began to creep and I scrambled out from under it.

"You didn't ask her properly," Bea hissed. "You didn't say please."

"Well you ask her."

"It's not me who wants the story, is it?"

"But you said to ask. I was asking for you."

"Shhh." Our mother leaned over from the front seat. "You'll wake Danny. Come and sit with me and I'll read you both a story."

NOW TRY THIS

It's time to read through your chosen text and write these basic notes. Your teacher may give you a date by which you should finish your notes. If this happens the teacher will probably ask you to hand these notes in for him or her to see.

Finding an angle

Once you have your basic notes it's time to work out your **angle**. In other words, you have to work out **what makes the text worth studying**.

When we study a text, most of what we might analyse fits into these five areas.

- **Plot** – what happens in the text, in the order it happens.

- **Character** – the people in the text, usually focusing on main or important or interesting characters.

- **Setting** – where and/or when the text happens.

- **Theme** – the ideas the author is trying to explore, the issues he or she wants readers to think about or learn about.

- **Style** – any particular features or techniques that the writer deliberately uses in the text.

So let's use those headings and some questions that go with them, to help you narrow down your angle of study.

NOW TRY THIS

You will need a photocopy of the following three pages. For each of the five areas listed above you'll find a few questions. First of all, read back over the notes you made about your text. Then answer the questions by filling in the boxes on your photocopy.

You should try quite hard to answer each question, but you may not actually end up with an answer for every one. As long as you have some answers by the end of the exercise, you'll have begun to narrow down your angle.

Is there **anything unusual about the plot**? For example, does the writer use any of the following techniques? Tick if you found any of these:

A **flashback**, when we are taken suddenly back to earlier events. ☐

A **turning point**, after which everything is different for the characters, or the story goes off in a different mood or direction. ☐

A **twist or shock**, when something really unexpected happens. ☐

A **climax** which the story builds up to, perhaps where the action becomes very dramatic, angry or even violent. ☐

If you have ticked any of the boxes above, use the next box to make brief notes about what it was you found interesting.

Who was the main **character** in your text?

Describe that person, especially their personality, by using a few key phrases.

Does this person change, grow, or develop over the course of the text? If so, how? Does he or she learn a lesson? If so what?

Name:_____ Class:_____

Was there another character you found particularly interesting? Who was it, and why were you interested?

```




```

Is there an important relationship, or important conflict between two (or more) characters in this text? If so, outline it briefly.

```




```

Does the text have a **setting** that is especially well-described or brought to life? If so, what is it? What makes the description so good?

```




```

Does the setting affect or change the characters or the plot? If so, how?

```




```

Can you identify one or two important **themes** in this text? What is it? / What are they?

```




```

How does the author mainly show this/these theme(s)?

```




```

Name:_____ Class:_____

Does the writer use any of these **aspects of style**? Tick if you found any of these:

Humour ☐

Similes, metaphors or other images ☐

Deliberately breaking any of the usual rules ☐

Creating a particular point of view ☐

Using hints, or only gradually revealing something ☐

Contrast ☐

Using lots of slang, or swearing, or special jargon ☐

Did you notice anything else in the writer's style that seemed to be deliberate or special? If so, what?

```



```

Did you notice anything else about the text that seemed to be important?

```



```

You should be much closer now to working out what makes the book worth studying. Read back over what you have written in all these boxes. You may also want to re-read your book notes one more time. Then answer the question below:

Which aspect of this text would you like to write about in your Personal Study?

```



```

Turning the angle into a title

You won't be able to do this bit until you have chosen an angle of study. If you have not yet found an angle then you may need help to do so. Make an appointment to see your teacher. Take along all the notes you've made so far. Your teacher should be able to suggest an angle, or to help you work one out. Once you have an angle, you can turn it into a title for your Study.

This title should show right away that you are going to be really studying and analysing your text, not just writing about it. The biggest danger students face when tackling this task is that they will just end up rehashing the plot, with an introduction and conclusion tacked on at the start and end of the Study.

You have already done a great deal to avoid that danger, because your notes and your answers to the last three pages of questions have helped you to find out what makes your chosen text worthy of study in the first place. The next thing you can do to help yourself is to give yourself a title that shows that your work is analytical.

There are three things you should put in that title:

1. the name of the text

2. the name of the author

3. the aspect of the text which you have chosen to study.

It's also a really good idea to begin your title with the words:

> *A study of how* (NAME OF AUTHOR)…

or

> *A study of* (NAME OF AUTHOR)'s…

That way you are making it clear from the outset that you are studying the text, not just writing about it, and that you are looking at the skills and techniques of the author.

To make that clear, let's go back to that student working on the novel *Hideous Kinky*, which was listed earlier in the chapter. We've already seen how she began her notes about the book and looked at her text marking on the first page of the book. Here's her title:

NOW TRY THIS

You are going to see a list of personal study titles. They are all based on novels from the list of suggestions earlier in the chapter. Read the titles. Decide for each of them whether the pupil is concentrating on plot, character, setting, theme, or some particular aspect of the writer's chosen style.

1. A study of how Douglas Adams examines human nature in the novel *The Hitch Hiker's Guide to the Galaxy*
2. A study of how Jake Arnott depicts Harry Stark in the novel *The Long Firm*
3. A study of how Pat Barker shows the ways war affects different people in the novel *Regeneration*
4. A study of how Christopher Brookmyre breaks the usual rules of thriller writing in the novel *A Big Boy Did It And Ran Away*
5. A study of how Harper Lee shows different forms of prejudice in the novel *To Kill a Mockingbird*
6. A study of the contrasting characters of the four boys in Stephen King's novel *The Body*
7. A study of how Philip Pullman creates a familiar but unfamiliar setting in the novel *Northern Lights*
8. A study of how Ian Rankin depicts Inspector Rebus in the novel *Knots and Crosses*.
9. A study of how Holden Caulfield relates to the different people he meets in J.D. Salinger's novel *Catcher in the Rye*
10. A study of how Muriel Spark shows Miss Brodie's good and bad sides in the novel *The Prime of Miss Jean Brodie*
11. A study of how Christopher tells us his own story in the novel *The Curious Incident of The Dog in the Night-Time* by Mark Haddon
12. A study of Paula's strengths and weaknesses in the novel *The Woman Who Walked Into Doors* by Roddy Doyle

13. A study of what William Golding is saying about human nature through the novel *Lord of the Flies*
14. A study of the relationship and conflict between the two boys in the novel *I'm the King of the Castle* by Susan Hill.
15. A study of violence, anger and aggression in the memoir *Jarhead* by Anthony Swofford

NOW TRY THIS

You've read your novel and made notes. You've answered questions to help you narrow down your angle. You've seen to how to construct a title and read 20 example titles. Now write the title for your Personal Study.

Keep a copy of the title for yourself, and then either give a note of your chosen title to your teacher or make an appointment to discuss that title. You shouldn't move on to the next stage until you are sure your teacher thinks you have made a good choice.

Planning your Personal Study

You should not write your Personal Study until you have written at least a couple of literature essays about texts that you have studied in class. That way you will be familiar with the structure for an essay, and with how to build paragraphs using the PEE technique.

All of that is covered in Chapter 9, so we are not going to say too much here about planning and writing your Study. A lot of what we do say here will also overlap with what you know or have done already.

Whatever your Study is about, at this stage you need to build yourself quite a detailed plan, fleshed out with notes and quotations.

Although Personal Studies can be, and often are, about plot, setting or an aspect of the writer's style, the majority of Intermediate 1 studies end up being about either character or theme. So we're going to take a bit of time to look here at how you might plan these types of Study.

Planning a study about theme

If you are writing about a theme, your plan can be a very straightforward one. You could set out your ideas in a table like the one below. This student is planning a Personal Study called:

A study of the theme of violence, anger and aggression in 'Jarhead' by Anthony Swofford

If you are going to use this kind of grid to plan your Study, you should try to write the 'event' section as a complete sentence. We'll see why that is in a moment.

Event in book	Evidence/Quotation	What this says about the theme
When Swofford's unit find out they are about to go to Iraq, they prepare by watching war movies.	*'For three days we … watch all of those damn movies … and we get off on the various visions of carnage and violence and deceit.' p5*	This shows that soldiers enjoy violence as an entertainment. They don't seem to be afraid of the violence of war.
In a break in the fighting, the men spend their time wrestling.	*'A recon sergeant has started a wrestling tournament … sand rises into a storm as snipers from all over the corps wrestle and cheer their fellows.' p154*	Again we see how much they enjoy aggression. They'd rather wrestle and fight than doing anything else in their spare time.

Just in case you're planning to write that Study, the example only has a couple of rows filled in. You should be able to fill in about three more, using this as a pattern. Altogether you need about five rows in your table, so that you are planning for five paragraphs in the main body of your Study.

Planning a study about character

Planning this sort of study is a little more complex, depending on what sort of character study you are doing.

Here's the plan for a student who is writing this Personal Study:

A study of how Muriel Spark shows Miss Brodie's good and bad sides in the novel 'The Prime of Miss Jean Brodie'

If you are going to use this sort of grid to plan your Study, you should try to write the 'aspect' section as a complete sentence. We'll see why that is in a moment.

Aspect of character	Evidence/quotation
Good: She totally devotes herself to her pupils.	She says, '*You girls are my vocation*', and that she would not marry and leave school even if someone proposed to her tomorrow. p23
Good:	
Good:	
Bad: She's fascinated by Nazis and Fascists and doesn't realise they are wrong or wicked.	The only bad thing she says about them is after the war when she admits, '*Hitler was rather naughty.*' p 122
Bad:	
Bad:	

Just in case you're planning to write that Study, the example only has one row filled in for each side of Miss Brodie. You should be able to fill in the rest, using this as a pattern.

You might be writing a Study about **the contrast between two characters**. Here's the plan for a student writing this Study:

A study of the contrast between Jack and Ralph in 'Lord of the Flies' by William Golding

If you are going to use this sort of grid to plan your Study, you should try to write the 'aspect' section as a complete sentence. We'll see why that is in a moment.

Aspect of character	Evidence/quotation
Jack doesn't want to listen to anyone else's opinion.	The first time he meets Piggy he soon says to him, *'You're talking too much ... shut up Fatty.'* p16
Jack:	
Jack:	
Ralph is sensitive to other people's feelings.	He understands that Jack is upset not to be voted leader at the start of the book, so he puts him in charge of the choir and makes them responsible for hunting.
Ralph:	
Ralph:	

Just in case you're planning to write that Study, the example only has one row filled in for each boy. You should be able to fill in the rest, using this as a pattern.

Using PEE to plan all sorts of studies

So now you've seen some models you might want to use to plan certain sorts of Personal Study. However, you can use the PEE paragraph structure to plan any Study at all.

You've met this structure already in Chapter 9, but here's a very quick reminder:

P – tells you to make a point which is relevant to your essay topic

E – tells you to give evidence from the text by quoting from or by referring to the text

E – tells you to explain the effect of this, to show what the writer is doing to us.

If you are going to use the PEE structure to plan your Study, you should try to write the P section as a complete sentence. We'll see why that is soon. For the moment, here's a PEE plan for the following Personal Study:

A study of how Christopher tells us his own story in the novel 'The Curious Incident of the Dog in the Night-Time' by Mark Haddon

Point	Evidence	Effect
Christopher retells conversations he has had accurately, but in a very dull way.	When he retells conversations he keeps using, 'And I said … And he said,' over and over, e.g. p7, p22, p94	This shows that he can't understand the emotions people feel when they speak. He can't describe moods or tones in voices, he just knows they spoke to him.
Sometimes Christopher explains exactly how his mind works.	'My memory is like a film. That is why I am really good at remembering things.' p96	He must know that he is unusual, and he seems to explain these things. He wants us to understand him, or even to realise how special he is.

Just in case you're planning to write that Study, the example only has a couple of rows filled in. You should be able to fill in about three more rows, using this as a pattern. Altogether you need about five rows in your table, so that you are planning for five paragraphs in the main body of your Study.

NOW TRY THIS

It's time to plan the main body of your study. Whichever way you do it, you need to have a plan that will give the Study about five main body paragraphs.

Take a blank piece of paper, lay it out to suit you chosen title, and plan your Study now.

NOW TRY THIS

Once you've written your plan, read it over. Ask yourself:

- Do I have **four or five clear points** to make?
- Is the first column of my plan all written in **whole sentences**?
- Does my plan show that I am really going to **analyse** my text, and look at the writer's skills and techniques?

Your teacher may wish to see the plan when it's finished.

The introduction and summary

By the time you write your Personal Study, you should already have had the opportunity to write at least a couple of essays about the literature you have studied in class. This means that you should already be quite confident about writing essay introductions, and that it should be easy for you to write a short summary of your chosen text. Remember – you can also look again at Chapter 9 of this book which deals with how to write literature essays.

However, just to save you flipping backwards and forwards through this book, here's a quick reminder. The following three things should appear in the introduction:

1. the title of the text you read

2. the name of the author who wrote this text

3. a clear indication of what you will be writing about.

After the introduction, it's a good idea to write a **short** summary of your text. This summary will give your teacher a little bit of context and background, making it easier for him or her to understand comments you make about your chosen text. Remember to keep it brief.

The introduction and summary might be two very short paragraphs, or you might find that what you want to say fits together better in one slightly longer one. Whether you do produce one paragraph or two at this stage, what you write should very closely fit your chosen task and title.

Have a look at this example. Here's the task this pupil has chosen:

A study of how Holden Caulfield relates to the different people he meets in J.D. Salinger's novel 'Catcher in the Rye'.

This is how this pupil's introduction and summary turned out:

> J.D. Salinger's novel 'Catcher in the Rye' is narrated to us by Holden Caulfield. He has been expelled from school and is making his way home to New York to tell his parents the bad news. On his journey he meets all sorts of different people, including old friends, total strangers, nuns and a prostitute. The different ways he relates to these people actually show us a lot about Holden himself, and they help us to understand the stressed any unhappy state he's in.

You've just seen an example of a good introduction and summary. Now you're going to see a bad one. The pupil has chosen this title for her study:

A study of how and why Robert Swindells uses two different narrators in his novel Stone Cold.

So far, so good. However, this is the way her Personal Study begins:

> *Link (that's not his real name but he never tells us what he's really called) is sixteen and he tells us about his life. He doesn't get on with his mum's new boyfriend Vince and he ends up living rough in Bradford. Then he gets fed up of people he knows seeing him, so he goes to London. He makes friends with Ginger who teaches him how to survive on the streets but then one day Ginger disappears. Soon after this Link meets Gail who is a homeless girl and he falls in love with her. Link and Gail go everywhere together. They gradually realise that lots of homeless people are going missing. They don't know it is Shelter but we do. Shelter is not his real name either. He used to be a soldier but he got put out of the army for health reasons. I think that he was a bit mental. He writes his daily routine orders about how he gets homeless people to come back to his flat and then he kills them and puts their bodies under the floor so they can be in his army. He nearly kills Link at the end but Gail arrives just in time but she is not who Link thought she was. She is a reporter and Link is safe but she is not in love with him and he is alone on the streets again.*

This opening has far too much plot, and it misses out some of the things that should appear at the start of any essay.

NOW TRY THIS

Can you rewrite the above opening and make it better?

Topic sentences

A few pages ago, when you were making your plan for the main body of your Study, you were told to make sure that certain parts of that plan were written in whole sentences. This is because we are going to use those as the **topic sentences** to begin each of these paragraphs when you write them.

You should remember reading about *topic sentences* in Chapter 9. Remember, they are called topic sentences for two reasons. Firstly, *they tie in with the topic of your essay*. Secondly, *they let the reader understand the topic of the paragraph you're on*.

NOW TRY THIS

Look back at your plan for the main body of your Study. Could you use the words in the first column of your plan as topic sentences to begin each paragraph in the main body? If you can, you're nearly ready to start writing. If you can't, then you need to rewrite those now so that you do have a set of topic sentences for those main body paragraphs.

The conclusion

There's just one more thing you need to think about before you can actually write your Personal Study. You need to decide what you want to say in your conclusion.

You should know from your essay-writing experience so far that you have to do two things:

1. Sum up and round off what you have written.

2. Give your personal response.

Summing up just means reminding the marker (your teacher) what you have written about. Giving your personal response takes a little more thought. At Intermediate level your personal response, just like everything else in your essay, should fit your chosen task, as well as fitting the text you are writing about. There's more about this in Chapter 9.

NOW TRY THIS

Believe it or not, even though you haven't yet written your whole essay, you should be able to write your conclusion. After all, you know your text very well and you have a very detailed essay plan, which means you actually know the material for your essay very well too. Write your conclusion now. Your teacher may wish to see it.

Writing your Personal Study

Controlled conditions

When it comes to eventually writing your piece, this has to be done under what is called **controlled conditions**. This means that you will have to work on your own. You'll be asked to sit alone and not to talk to anyone else while you do your writing. You'll have to be well prepared because once you begin to write you won't be able to ask your teacher or anyone else for help or advice.

You can use your copy of the text. Did you remember to mark it up with highlights, underlining and notes? You can use your plan for the body paragraphs, and you can also use the introduction, summary and conclusion you have written already. You won't be allowed to use a dictionary or thesaurus. You will have about an hour to write your piece of work.

What to do

First of all, neatly write out your introduction and summary. Then, following your plan, write the main body of the essay. This should consist of four or five paragraphs. Each paragraph should follow the PEE structure and should begin with one of the topic sentences you write for yourself. Finish your essay by adding the conclusion you have prepared already.

NOW TRY THIS

When you've finished, read your work over before you hand it in to your teacher. Think about the four areas you will be assessed on and ask yourself the following questions:

Understanding
- Have I shown that I understand my chosen text?
- Have I referred to the text to back up the points I make?

Analysis
- Have I analysed how the writer writes, and not just retold the story?

Evaluation
- Have I shown my personal response?
- Have I given evidence to show why I responded this way?

Expression
- Are my spelling, grammar and punctuation good?
- Is my point of view clear?

What happens next?

Your teacher will now spend some time reading and marking your Personal Study. If your Study is written well enough, and if you show enough evidence of each of the four skills, then that's it. You've passed and you don't need to look at the Personal Study again.

If you have not passed, your teacher should give you some advice, either in writing or in person, to explain how your study can be improved. The good news is that you do not need to start again from the beginning with a new book. You should only need to rewrite parts of your study. Your teacher will tell you when he or she wants you to do the rewrite, which again should be done in school under controlled conditions. Make sure you understand what you have to do to be able to pass second time round – you won't be able to ask once you start writing.

11 The Writing NAB

One of the four assessments, or NABs, that you have to pass in school before the exam is to produce your own piece of original writing. This chapter will help you to prepare and write it.

What the markers are looking for

How do the examiners want you to tackle this writing task? What do they want you to prove about your skills?

They are actually looking at four different areas of your writing skill: **content**, **structure**, **expression** and **technical accuracy**.

- Your **content** should be relevant to the writing task you are doing. It should be suitable for the audience who will read it. You should develop a number of different points or ideas.

- Your piece should have good **structure**. It should be organised, straightforward, and clear to follow. The structure should suit your chosen task and suit the likely audience who will read what you write.

- In your **expression** you should use the techniques we expect to find in your chosen genre of writing. (For example, if you choose to write a story, you will need to develop characters and give them dialogue to speak, and the story will need a good plot with a beginning, middle and end.) If you are doing personal reflective writing you should follow the guidelines in this chapter about how to produce that kind of writing. You need to choose suitable words and vary the types of sentences you use. The reader should be able to recognise your point of view in what you write.

- **Technical accuracy** is how well you use the English language in your writing. This includes your spelling, grammar and punctuation. These should all be accurate.

Your final piece of writing has to pass **in all four** of these areas. Every one of the four aspects must be handled well enough to satisfy the marker.

Content	✓	Structure	✓	Expression	✓	Technical accuracy	✓

The good news is that, because this is a NAB and not an exam task, the marker will be your English teacher and you should know the result pretty quickly. Also, again because this is a NAB, if you don't pass first time you will receive feedback about your work and have the opportunity to try again. However, if you work your way through this chapter carefully, you shouldn't need to have two goes at it.

Working conditions

There should be time in class for you to learn about the particular skills needed for the kind of writing task you are going to work on. You should get a chance to discuss what you are going to write about, and to make a plan.

When it comes to eventually writing your piece, this has to be done under what is called **controlled conditions**. This means that you will have to work on your own. You'll be asked to sit alone and not to talk to anyone else while you do your writing. You'll have to be well prepared because once you begin to write you won't be able to ask your teacher or anyone else for help or advice. You also won't be allowed to use anything to help you – no dictionary or thesaurus. You will have about an hour to write your piece of work. This may all sound very tough, but remember this all comes after lots of preparation time. Also, when you pass you will have the satisfaction of knowing you really deserved to.

Different types of writing

There are several different genres, or types of writing, which you can choose for this NAB. You may write an essay in which you give information about some subject you know well. You could produce a piece of discursive writing, in which you handle ideas and opinions. You could write persuasively, hoping to convince the reader to agree with your views on some topic. Or you could produce a piece of Personal Reflective writing. All these options are open to you, but in this book we are going to concentrate on only one of them: **Personal Reflective Writing**.

You are most likely to do really well in the essay writing NAB if you choose to produce a piece of personal reflective writing. Why do you think this is?

NOW TRY THIS

Work with a partner, a small group, or with your class. Make a list of all the reasons you can think of to explain why people do best at this type of writing.

Choosing what to write about

You know that at the end of this course, in the exam, you will write two essays about literature. You will have to choose these two essay tasks from a list of six possible ones printed in the exam paper.

This essay, the Personal Reflective one, is a bit different. You should be able to choose your own essay topic and turn that into a title. (This isn't the only time in Intermediate 1 that you'll have to do this. You have to find your own title for your Personal Study of Literature too. You can find out all about that in Chapter 10 of this book.)

It shouldn't be too hard for you to choose a topic. After all, you know yourself better than anyone else does. Only you have lived your life. You are the only person in the world who has had your

particular set of experiences. You are the only person in history who ever had the exact set of family and friends that you have. Your brain is the only one in the entire universe to hold your set of memories, thoughts and feelings. You are unique, and you are important. You are well worth writing about.

NOW TRY THIS

Stop right now and have a think. Is there a personal experience you have had which matters to you very much, one that you'd like to write about in your Personal Reflective essay? If there is, write it down on a piece of paper now and put that paper somewhere safe.

Narrowing down your ideas

If you don't have a subject in mind already, then it may help you to think very quickly about a lot of different experiences you may have had, and see if any of them are suitable for you to write a longer piece about.

NOW TRY THIS

You'll see one question which splits into five parts. Can you write just one paragraph for each option below? What is the:

- worst ■ hardest ■ happiest ■ saddest ■ most frightening thing that has ever happened to you?

NOW TRY THIS

This time the question splits into six parts. Can you write just one paragraph for each option below? Which event or time in your life:

- has most shaped you
- has made you grow up or mature
- has most changed your family
- has been most confusing
- showed you the best of people/someone
- showed you the worst of people/someone?

NOW TRY THIS

Now you are going to think about some ways a person could make an impact on your life. Again, can you write just one paragraph for each option below? Which person:

- has most influenced you
- has most helped you
- has most hurt you
- do you miss most
- are you most glad to be rid of?

You should now have anything up to sixteen short paragraphs in front of you. Read them over. One or two of them may be especially good. Perhaps there were some you wished you could have written much more about, because you felt you had a lot more to say.

NOW TRY THIS

Stop now and have a think. Is there a paragraph which got you writing about something which matters to you very much, something that you'd like to write about in your Personal Reflective essay? If there is, write it down on a piece of paper now and put that paper somewhere safe.

Some possible tasks

If all of that still hasn't given you an idea of something you'd like to write about, you'll see a list of tasks below. In each one, the main thing you have to write about is printed in **bold**. The following advice in plain type is to help you plan your writing. It will remind you about the thoughts feelings, details, description and reflection that you need to use all the way through.

- **Write about a person who has had a great impact on your life.** Give a clear description of that person's looks and personality. Show how this person made an impact on your life, perhaps at a particular time. Go on to reflect on how much you still feel that impact today.

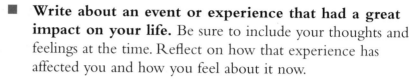

- **Write about an event or experience that had a great impact on your life.** Be sure to include your thoughts and feelings at the time. Reflect on how that experience has affected you and how you feel about it now.

- **Write about a relationship that has changed greatly, either for the worse or for the better.** If it is relevant, explain how the relationship first began. Make clear what the relationship was like before the change, and what caused that change. What is the relationship like now? Do you think it might change again in the future? Use thoughts and feelings throughout. Reflect on what you have learned about yourself, and about the other person (or people) involved.

- **Write about a time when you felt isolated.** Explain the circumstances that led you to feel this way, how you handled the experience at the time and how it has gone on to affect you.

- **Write about a time when you were in conflict with someone over a particular issue.** Be sure to include your thoughts and feelings at the time. Reflect on how that conflict has affected you and how you feel about it now.

- **Write about a time when you lost someone or something special.** Deal with your thoughts and feelings at the time of the loss. Make it clear how you felt then and why. Through reflection, show how you feel now about this loss.

- **Write about a time when you experienced personal success.** Concentrate on your thoughts and feelings at the time. Make sure you reflect on how that success has changed or affected you.

- **Write about a time when you were given some responsibility.** Write about how you carried that out at the time and show what you thought and felt. Did you handle that responsibility well or badly? Reflect on what you learned or gained from having this responsibility.

Good writing techniques

Thoughts and feelings

Your Personal Writing will really come to life when you include your thoughts and feelings. No one else knows these. Only you can tell the reader what was happening in your mind and heart.

Interestingly, people often write extremely well about the hardest events in life. If we go through sad, difficult or tragic events we are strongly aware of how we feel at the time. Also, while a happy event in the end may just become a happy memory, sad events affect and shape us. We have to keep working with and processing the memories, thoughts and feelings that go with these events.

Let's look at an example. The writer, Oscar Moore, had been seriously ill. One side-effect of his illness was that he began to go blind. This extract describes his mixed feelings just after an operation to restore his eyesight.

I slipped into sleep and awoke the following morning in a disoriented daze. Stupid with sleep, I forgot I had a bandage over my seeing eye and fear rose like ice in my veins as I tried to make sense of a world that consisted of shades of grey. A nurse came and led me to the other end of the ward where the surgeon was waiting. As I sat there, silent with terror, he unwrapped my unthinking head and left me blinking in dazed and grinning confusion. Admittedly everything was a little fuzzy, but it was in colour and I could tell who were people and what were machines.

The operation had been a success, he said.

I ambled gingerly back to my room and ran a bath. Then, just as I was used to being waited on, a friend came to collect me. I hadn't really thought about anything beyond the immediate. But, muttering darkly and peering gloomily, I was shepherded into a cab and taken home.

When someone brought me a pot of tea and a cup, I carefully poured the tea out on to the table next to the cup, scalding my legs and chilling my mind.

I felt stupid, desperate, alone, and scared.

I wanted to scream and shout. I wanted peace and quiet. I wanted everyone to leave. I wanted everyone to stay. I wanted help. I didn't want to be crowded.

NOW TRY THIS

Moore is obviously feeling a mixture of emotions, some positive, some negative. Copy and complete the following table to help you explore the emotions in the extract.

Emotion	Evidence	Positive or negative?
Fear	*'Fear rose like ice in my veins'*	Negative

When you write about your own thoughts and feelings, don't just state what these were, but explore them too. Don't just tell the reader you were angry, but say why, and how that anger felt. Don't just tell the reader you were afraid, but say why, and show how that fear affected you.

Details and descriptions

NOW TRY THIS

Think of a strong memory. Now close your eyes for 30 seconds and think about it again.

Could you see it? Could you hear it? Was there a smell, a taste or a texture?

Because your memories are important to you, when you bring them to mind they will be full of tiny details, things you noticed at the time. Many of these details might not be very important in themselves, but they become important because they bring that memory to life.

The following extract from Ellen McCarthur's autobiography is an example of such details. At the age of 28 she made the fastest ever solo sailing trip around the world. Her interest in boats began while she was still at school, as this piece of writing shows.

I had worked out that it was going to take a lot more than birthday and Christmas money to save for a boat. The only other source of income that passed through my hands was school dinner money, and once I was at secondary school this vital source of cash came under my control rather than being paid in at the beginning of each week. I started a new regime which lasted until I finally left school. I would take a couple of slices of bread and a tomato or banana from the cupboard when I left home in the morning, then collect apples, plums or pears from the garden for lunch. My other option during the fruitless winter months was to buy mashed potato and beans, which cost just 8 pence, then smother it with gravy, which was free. A special treat would be a jacket potato and baked beans (24 pence) though that was a fairly rare occurrence. Every night I would religiously pile up the coins on top of my money box, marking off a square each time I made £1.

This short passage is stuffed with tiny details. We know exactly what sort of food she took from the kitchen, which fruit grew in the garden, and the cost of different school dinners. We know where she kept her cash. Did you notice the odd detail that she put the coins *on top* of her money box, rather than inside it? We even know how she kept track of her savings.

NOW TRY THIS

Read the following extract from Andrea Ashworth's book, *Once in a House on Fire*. As you read it, make a list of the small details which make it seem vivid and convincing.

Laurie and I were zipped nose to nose into an itchy sleeping bag on the settee while our bedroom was stripped and decorated. Our stepfather hired a bearded man who looked like Jesus to paste up the new wallpaper, but soon caught him using our telephone to make secret, long-distance calls. He dragged the man outside and punched him in the street, shoved him into his car and slammed the door on his foot. The car dribbled off with the driver's nose bleeding into his moustache, the half-used cans of paint wobbling on the back seat. My stomach churned because I was the one who had blabbed about the calls.

Being reflective

So far in looking at using thoughts, feelings, details and descriptions, we have been concentrating on the basic skills of Personal Writing. However, you will remember that this task is not called just *Personal Writing* but *Personal **Reflective** Writing*. To be able to do this task well and to pass it, you need to write **reflectively**. This is something that only mature and insightful writers are able to do. But what does it mean?

It means two things at once.

If you stand in front of a mirror you can examine yourself pretty thoroughly by looking at your reflection. Every spot and blemish will be visible, but you'll also be able to see all your good features and everything that you like about yourself.

That's the first meaning of being reflective in Writing – examining yourself. You might question and criticise yourself. On the other hand you might affirm yourself and realise that you handled the situation well. You may realise that certain experiences have shaped you and made you into the person you are, just as growing up changes the way your face looks in the mirror.

Now think of the rear-view mirror in a car. The driver can keep his or her eyes on the road ahead, while using the mirror to see what is happening behind.

That's the second meaning of being reflective in Writing – looking back. Often events in our lives make much more sense once they are over and we are older and wiser. Perhaps when something happened to you it was a really terrible experience, but now you realise that you benefited from it in some way. Events may be confusing when they happen, but when you look back on them they may make more sense.

Of course, as well as reflecting on yourself you can reflect on others. You can question the way people behaved, or show that you understand now why they did the things they did. It may be that you disagreed with someone at the time, but you now realise they did the right thing. On the other hand, when we are young we sometimes accept the things adults do without question, but as we grow up we are not so sure about their motives. You may also be aware of how events and experiences have affected other people as well as yourself.

Below is a list of reflective phrases. Any of these phrases can be used to begin a reflective sentence or a reflective paragraph. In fact if you use one of them, whatever you write in the rest of the paragraph will definitely be reflective.

Looking back…	Because of this I am…
On reflection…	Since this happened I…
With hindsight…	When I think back on this…
In retrospect…	Thinking about it now I feel…
Nowadays I feel/think/believe…	At the time I … but now I…
If I could do this again…	If I could change things…
If this happened now…	It was a … thing to do because…
I learned…	I wish this had never happened because…
I realise…	Now that I've been through this…
I understand…	I grew through this experience because…
I should have…	This experience has shaped me by…
I could have…	I'm glad this happened because…
I wish I had…	

Looking at some real examples

You are going to see two pieces of reflective writing produced by real pupils. Both writers were aged about sixteen when they wrote these. Their essays are excellent examples of the kind of thing that someone around your age can actually write.

NOW TRY THIS

First of all just read through the two pieces of writing. You may wish to do this aloud around the class, or you might want to read them on your own.

In Flanders Field

Many a brave man fought and died for his country. It took me and my classmates five days away in France and Belgium exploring the battlefields of World War One to actually realise how brave and dedicated to their country these men really were. I thought at the start of my journey that it would be a good memorable trip away with my friends. I was right, a little bit. I was with my friends and it was memorable. Never did I think it was going to change the way I felt about World War One's heart-breaking history.

I'd always known that poppies were associated with war, but never knew why. The first place my classmates and I visited was a place called Ypres in Belgium. Ypres was the death place of John McCrae, who wrote a poem called 'In Flanders Fields'.

As I sat beside a memorial for John McCrae I gazed off at the huge field that seemed to go on for many miles. As our tour went on to tell us what the field used to be and who John McCrae was I had a tear in my eye and a lump in my throat. It was hard for me to sit there staring at a field that had been a battlefield. In my head I could just see all the soldiers running into battle. This is what McCrae did. He sat in the spot where I was now sitting and wrote a poem. I felt so privileged to be sitting in the same place as him.

> 'In Flanders Fields the poppies blow
> Between the crosses row on row…
> We are the dead, short days ago,
> We lived and saw sunset glow,'

was part of McCrae's poem that became famous during 1916. From then on poppies have been worn as a sign of respect for the men who gave up their lives.

Hearing that poem made me glad that nowadays a great war like World War One is unlikely to happen, but at the same time it helped me to realise that although the men are dead I still need to remember them. I'm so proud to wear a poppy on my chest.

We all visited many different places. The one I've just written about and the next one I'm going to write about are the two that stuck in my head the most. The reason for this is that I'm a very emotional person and they both made a great dent in my way of thinking.

I was at the back of everyone else. I just couldn't stand at the front anymore. It was too upsetting for me. I was crying, why? I didn't even know the boy. The gravestone, white as snow read:

'Unknown but to God, aged 16, may he rest in peace'.

Reading 'Unknown but to God' was the reason I felt great sympathy towards this boy. Who was he? Why was he so young? All these questions ran through my head as I sobbed.

I was so grateful when we left the graveyard of the youngest boy to die in World War One. I was sixteen too. I wasn't ready to die and didn't want to either, but he had, he had gone forever. But why? I could never be as brave as so many of these men were. That's what in my head it all boils down to.

'In life we hardly knew you, in death we'll never forget you'

was what our poppy wreath said. It was true for so many of us, especially me. By the end of the trip, I became quite quiet because there were so many feelings running through my head. I'd seen over 100,000 gravestones and I just needed time to think.

Now it's almost five months on and I still have very clear images of the graves in my head. I feel that the trip has made me a better person, because now I understand the full concept of war, hurt and guilt.

My Cousin Sophie

We all look at stick thin models and want to have their perfect bodies. We do everything to look just like them: Yoga, swimming, dieting the lot, but somehow we just can't see ourselves like that. We look in the mirror and see fat ugly monsters staring back at us.

My cousin Sophie was never very confident about her weight. I kept telling her how perfect she was but she wouldn't listen. She did every exercise you could think of and went on every diet there was, but she still saw herself as fat. I often wondered why she was so self-conscious. After all, she was only a size ten.

After a couple of months Sophie started to look thinner. Everyone kept saying she was. Looking back now I wish I had stopped her, if only I knew.

Her mum would phone my mum and tell her how Sophie always looked so tired or how Sophie had failed yet another test. As I listened on the other line I found this very strange. Sophie was a happy, bright, intelligent girl.

After that my curiosity got the better of me and I started to listen in on every conversation they had. Each phone call seemed to get worse and worse. Sophie's mum would say 'Oh but she is getting so thin,' or, 'Oh Sophie never ate her dinner again tonight.' Nowadays I feel that my auntie should have forced the food down her throat, but I realise Sophie would only have put up a fight.

Before Sophie stopped eating we were very close, but the thinner she got the more we grew apart. Now I feel I should have been there for her but no one was to know how much danger she was putting herself in.

Her mum came home from work one day to find Sophie lying on the couch with no life about her at all. She was rushed to hospital. The doctors diagnosed her with an eating disorder. My heart sank, as the doctors explained she could die in a matter of months or even weeks. My body started shaking, I froze, and I could hear everyone around me crying and the doctor's voice in the background.

I sneaked out of the waiting room so that no one would notice I was away. I slowly opened the door to the room where my cousin was lying on a bed. There she was thinner than a stick, as white as a ghost, lifeless. I didn't say anything. I just watched over her fragile body. All I could hear was my breathing and hers. For some reason I blamed myself that she was this way. I questioned myself. Did she do it because she was being bullied? Was it my fault I didn't stay close to her? I still have all these questions spinning in my mind.

After Sophie had been in hospital for over three months she was finally allowed home. I was so happy she was getting better, she was going to live. She took me out shopping and we had a wonderful time. I knew at that moment the old Sophie was back. She was still very thin but we all knew it would take time.

On the 18th of November that year Sophie was found in her bed, dead. The whole family was in complete shock, including me. We all thought she had got better. Yet again the same questions came spinning in my head. Why her? How could this have happened?

When I look back now I see very bad memories of the day I saw her lying in the hospital bed, but I try and think of the better memories of how she always used to find something to do if we were bored. She had a lovely funeral service and I will always remember her. She wasn't just my cousin, she was my best friend too.

NOW TRY THIS

Now that you have read the stories once, you are going to analyse them in more detail. The easiest way to do this is to have a photocopy of each story in front of you. You'll also need pens, pencils or highlighters in three different colours. You may wish to work with a partner to do the following things as you read the stories again:

1. Every time you find the writer sharing their **thoughts** or **feelings**, underline or highlight that part of the story in your first colour.
2. Every time you find the writer using **detail** or **description**, underline or highlight that part of the story in your second colour.
3. Every time you find the writer **being reflective**, underline or highlight that part of the story in your third colour.
4. Write a couple of sentences for each piece to show what made it a **good** piece of writing.
5. For each piece, suggest two things the writer could have done that would have made their work **even better**.

Writing your piece

It's time for you to start writing your own piece of reflective writing. You should have decided by now what you want to write about. If you still haven't, you need to look back at the part of this chapter about making that choice.

First of all you need to make a plan.

NOW TRY THIS

Take a new sheet of paper, at least A4 size. At the top write the task you have chosen. The divide the rest of the page into four squares with headings as shown on the next page.

Now use the four squares to plan what you want to put into your piece of work. Remember: this is just the **plan**, not the writing itself. You don't need to write in whole sentences. Key words, phrases or bullet points will do fine. It's probably easiest if you start with the top left box, where you slot in the rough outline of the story that you're telling. Then go on and fill in the other boxes with the thoughts and feelings, details and description, and reflection you want to use.

Just in case that doesn't make sense, take a look at page 235. On it you'll see the planning sheet for the piece you've just read called *In Flanders Field*.

Your title goes here

The basic story

Start

Middle

End

Thoughts and feelings

Details and description

Reflection

In Flanders Field

The basic story

Start
Start At John McCrae's memorial

Middle
At the gravestone of the unknown 16-year-old

End
Leaving our poppy wreath

Thoughts and feelings

Nearly crying

Feeling privileged

Respect for men who fought

Proud now to wear a poppy

Sympathy for the very young dead soldier

Feeling I couldn't be as brave as them

Details and description
Huge field that seemed to go on for miles

Words of poem John McRae wrote

Description of 16-year-old's gravestone

Words on our poppy wreath

100,000 gravestones

Reflection

Didn't realise how brave these men were until I went to the battlefields

Memorable trip but not how I expected

I realised I had to remember these men

I'm an emotional person – I remember the things that made me feel something

Don't why I was crying because I didn't know the dead boy

The trip made me a better person

Of course there are other things in the piece of writing that aren't on this plan. Whatever you put on your plan has to be joined together with other material too. However, you should be able to see how a plan like this could help you get ready to do a really good piece of Personal Reflective Writing.

NOW TRY THIS

In peace and quiet, with your plan beside you, sit down and write your piece. This should take you around an hour to do.

NOW TRY THIS

When you've finished, read your work over before you hand it in to your teacher. Think about the four areas you will be assessed on and ask yourself the following questions:

Content
- Have I stuck to my task?
- Have I developed my ideas?

Structure
- Is my work organised, straightforward, and clear to follow?

Expression
- Have I followed the guidelines in this chapter about personal reflective writing?
- Have I used good vocabulary and different sorts of sentences?
- Is my point of view clear?

Technical accuracy
- Are my spelling, grammar and punctuation the best I can possibly achieve?

Once you have checked over your work, hand it in to your teacher. He or she will soon let you know whether you have passed this NAB first time round. If you haven't, your teacher should be able to tell you what to change so that you can pass on a second try. This may be written advice, or you may have a chance to discuss your work.